FREE ME FOREVER!

FREE ME FOREVER!

HOW I BOUGHT 29 HOUSES IN 24 MONTHS USING NONE OF MY OWN MONEY

KYLE P HARPER

This publication is designed to provide general information regarding the subject matter covered. However, laws and practices often vary from state to state and are subject to change. Because each factual situation is different, specific advice should be tailored to the particular circumstances. For this reason, the reader is advised to consult with his or her own advisor regarding that individual's specific situation.

This book is based on actual events; however, names have been changed.

The author has taken reasonable precautions in the preparation of this book and believes the facts presented in the book are accurate as of the date it was written. However, neither the author nor the publisher assume any responsibility for any errors or omissions. The author and publisher specifically disclaim any liability resulting from the use or application of the information contained in this book, and the information is not intended to serve as legal advice related to individual situations.

Free Me Forever! is a registered trademark of Free Me Forever, LLC.
ISBN: 0983403902
ISBN-13: 9780983403906
Library of Congress Control Number: 2011923876

This book is dedicated to my wife and best friend Sara.

I love you more than words can say. Thank you for your unconditional love and support through the valleys which enable us to always end up on top!

TABLE OF CONTENTS

PREFACE

Waiting for a call on a muggy Friday afternoon in coastal North Carolina, I finally heard the phone ring, but what I heard next was alarmingly unexpected. As Director of Marketing and Sales for a resort development, I collected money from developers; since we were in the start-up phase of our project, they relied upon bank draws to pay me. Picking up the phone, I assumed the developer was calling to deliver my check, as usual.

"Kyle, how was your week?" asked Bill.

Usually, Bill would have known exactly how my week had gone. For the previous two years, we had worked side-by-side 60 to 70 hours a week in bringing our project to life.

"Amazing!" I replied, still riding high on the buzz from the birth of my daughter; my first-born child had come into the world on Monday, only four days prior. In the delivery room with my wife and the doctor, I spent the entire eight hours holding a leg, coaching my wife and right before my eyes, life began! I saw the first breath, heard the first cry, and even cut with my own hands the connection from mother to child. So you can just imagine, I wasn't exaggerating when I said to Bill that I was having an "Amazing week; by far, the best and most amazing week of my life." Nor did I know how right I was.

"I'm glad you had a good week," Bill came back. "And I hate to tell you this now, but we don't have any money in the account."

Thinking it was probably just delayed as usual, I asked, "When do you think the bank will release the money?"

But the gravity of his tone spoke volumes when he replied, "I don't know. As of right now, it looks doubtful."

He was right; the money wasn't coming. Because of the tightening credit markets, the bank had begun refusing to release funds, cutting off the budget for marketing – namely, me.

During that phone call – those few seconds – my life changed forever. I felt crushed, terrified, powerless. How would I support my new family? My precious wife and girl depended on me, me *entirely*. How would I *ever* start back up in the worst housing market since the Great Depression? Wasn't I already a casualty of that nightmarish market?

In August, only a month before, the jumbo-loan crisis had struck, now marking the beginning of our current Great Recession. In those days everyone seemed to "know" only one thing: the market was terrible and looking worse every day.

Dazed and numb, that afternoon I sat with my mother-in-law and my exhausted wife – who, by this point, already hadn't slept for several nights – to explain to the two women what I had just heard from Bill. It felt like I was dreaming, like none of it was real; I remember wishing I would soon wake up to find myself comfortably asleep on my $10k monthly cushion. Any second, things would go back to normal; we'd all wake up from a nasty dream.

But it was no dream. Seriously stressing, we all sat in a quiet circle and, at the pit of despair, reflected on our doom.

I look back on that life-changing afternoon and realize that the job I thought I couldn't live without was, in reality, the only thing holding me back from truly living. Like a prisoner, I marched the same daily march through my habits, working almost every day, trading my time – the most precious thing we have – for money. Although I didn't realize it right away, Bill's phone call had snipped *my* umbilical cord, and like my daughter, *I* was beginning a new life. At that moment I had no idea, but Bill's news had freed me forever.

INTRODUCTION

This book aims to give you a glimpse into the freedom you can create for yourself when you take the right steps. In this book, you will learn the steps that I have taken to create wealth by purchasing 29 houses in 24 months using none of my own money. I will give you the details about what I did and how I did it. I will also go into the specifics of the different aspects of gaining success by utilizing the tools of my unique system.

While the general components of your journey may resemble mine, obviously you, taking a slightly different path than I, will get unique results. Remember: this is *your* journey to Freedom. Opportunities will present themselves to you that I never experienced. I will tell you every detail, every step that I took along the way, so that you can learn from my experience. Along the way, you will learn what works best for you, and what doesn't. You'll see how things don't always, in fact almost never, turn out just as you plan, but you will learn creative strategies for making your plan work. Of course, I don't expect (or even want) you to do exactly as I have done; the destiny you must fulfill is your own. What's important is to maintain a stance of openness and flexibility so that you can recognize and take advantage of the opportunities that arise during your journey.

The common elements we will share on our respective journeys include some fundamental steps. For instance, it will require decisiveness to overcome your fears when you purchase your first property. It will require persistence to overcome your self-doubts while trying to find your first source of funding. It will require courage to ask people to fund your projects. When you step up and begin to grow in these ways, and especially when the money starts flowing in, you will build greater confidence. Nothing compares to the confidence that comes with success, and nothing compares with the freedom you will feel when you achieve complete financial independence. At that point, no one can hold anything over your head. Without fear of repercussions from the top, you will have absolute freedom. You will *be* the top!

This book spells out a genuine journey to financial freedom. You will realize it lies within your power to create your own destiny and to provide for yourself without working your life away. This book will also challenge you to look deep inside yourself, to expose yourself. You will completely create and control your own life, and you will have no one besides yourself to take the credit or blame for the outcome. On the surface, this book is about becoming a millionaire in as little as two years through real estate investment – something anyone can do! And guess what? That's actually the easy part. Beneath the surface, this book is about releasing the person trapped within you right now; it's about setting free the part of you that wants to create your own life, a life of abundance, a life filled with money, time, and loving relationships.

The funny thing is you will realize the money that you set out to chase is the least important part when you succeed. The strong character that you develop and set free from within you is the true treasure. The part of you buried deep inside right now can't wait to be released. Deep inside, you know that you can become the person you have never even dared to dream about until now. I know. I recently walked in your shoes. Maybe even worse, I was unemployed with a new baby and scared to death. But facing my fears, facing my truth, I acknowledged my unlimited potential that only my fears held back. Now I realize that I can create any life I want. Today I recognize that the only things able to hold me back are my own perceptions of myself and the world around me. I embraced the truth, and the truth Freed Me Forever!

CHAPTER 1

WHY THIS BOOK?

Why should you read this book over the other books written about real estate investing? Because one thing is for sure: this is not *just* a book about real estate, written for investors. The subject matter of the book deals with real estate, since that's what I know, and it will teach you about real estate and how you can get started as an investor, but at its heart, this book is about knowing your options – knowing that you have options in investing, knowing that you have options for working, knowing that you have options for your family and for your life.

Too many of us assume that we must get a job, working for someone else's company to have a successful, secure life, only to find out that it causes undue stress, and after working our entire lives away, we end up with less than we need to live our "golden years" in comfort. Even worse, compared to how we dreamed of spending those golden years, we end up with *much* less. Corporate America has sold us on the idea that we need to keep our heads down, defer our wants in life until later on, and work through the best years of our lives, the best years of our *families'* lives, in order to sit back and live the good life when we retire. But what is the reality?

Reality: we work our lives away, spending all our energy making someone else rich, while we fall further and further behind. In reality, the financial planner taking care of your retirement is probably in the same situation as you, not a wealthy individual giving you advice, but a hungry salesperson trying to survive. Also in reality, a traditional 401k or IRA may or may not give you the money you need to retire. It will depend on how much you give, when you start giving, and mostly, where the market cycle is when you need the money. As we all know by now, the stock market does not always rise. Just like the real estate market, the stock market goes through cycles. This is fine if you can afford to leave the money alone during the low periods. In fact, it gives you a buying opportunity. However, things look worse if you are speculating on selling your investment to cover your living expenses.

The good news is that we all have choices. Nothing says we have to spend our entire lives working for someone else. We don't have to hand our money over to someone else to invest for us. We don't have to live the deferred life plan, which says we put off having fun until retirement. It's time we learn to see past these common, sad misconceptions.

If you are not living your life exactly how you want, then this book is for you. You should not have to wait another day before living life exactly how you choose. All you have is time, the great equalizer. Every person in the world has the same amount of time each day. Some people spend it accumulating a fortune, while others spend it working for those people. Which side would you rather be on? Every day you make that choice.

If you decide you want to take the present, and therefore the future, into your own hands, then this book will help. It will teach you how to face your fears, how to dream big, how to put a plan into action by working toward your ideal lifestyle, even if you don't know how you will get there. Your plan will change as you go down the road to your destiny.

I know this because of my own experience. At first, when I received the phone call that ended my job security, I made a choice because I thought it was the best way to provide for my family. Then as I started down the path of assembling my team and studying the market, I realized that there was something much bigger going on. I was going to be providing for my family, but I was also developing myself. I was learning how to live on my own and how to build an economic system for me and my family which was independent of others. I was learning business skills that would enable me to find my own way in the world and collect some of the trillions of dollars that trade hands around the world every day.

Once I had a system in place that I knew would provide the essentials, then I started asking questions that went beyond money. I started asking myself, *"Why do I do the things that I do? What is most important to me in life? How do I want to spend my time each day?"*

Asking these questions made a profound impact on my life. Up until that point, I had managed all my own properties. I was the one who signed all the leases, met the tenants, and fielded the maintenance calls. I was the one who marketed and sold the properties. Once I started asking myself these deep and personal questions, I realized I didn't want my kids to think of me as a great landlord, I wanted them to think of me as a great father. I didn't want my business associates to think of me as an efficient manager, I wanted them to think of me as an innovator. I didn't want my wife to think of me as a hard worker, I wanted her to think of me as a loving husband. I didn't want to spend my days becoming a better landlord, I wanted to spend my days becoming a better human being.

With this in mind, I hired property managers. Sure, it costs a little money, but in the long run, it enables me to achieve more and increase my overall worth, both monetarily and emotionally. That move set me free to follow my dreams to the next assumed peak. What I thought was a peak, financial independence, I soon realized was only a knoll. As I rose to the next peak of self-discovery on a journey that has led me to this moment, I began to feel the need to share this knowledge with you.

I don't remember where I heard this, but I always keep it in the back of my mind: someone said that you can only cut costs so much, but you can increase the top line indefinitely. In other words, if you focus on keeping your costs low, you can only attain a certain level of success since you can't drive your cost to $0, or to a negative number. However, you can increase the top line to infinity by increasing sales or creating a new product, therefore, attaining unlimited success. I live my life by this principle. If I focus too long on managing the details, then I realize I am only "cutting costs" when I should be creating either sales or a new product – expanding my consciousness. The details always work themselves out if I stay focused on the big picture.

If you have ever climbed a mountain or gone snow skiing, then you know as you climb or ride the lift, it seems like you see the peak. As you get closer and closer, higher and higher, you can see the clouds in the sky, you are almost there, and then you come over what you assumed to be the peak, and you see a whole new mountain rising before you: a new peak. You continue to rise, approaching the next assumed peak, only to find, once again, you are just seeing a knoll on the hill, not the peak at the top. Time and time again, as you continue, what you think is the peak, your ideal lifestyle when you begin, will be just a reflection point. Once you reach it, you will gain a new perspective on life. You will have a new appreciation for the people and relationships in your life, and as you rise, you will continually see new peaks. As you approach the next peak, your thoughts will change, your consciousness will change, your life will change, and you will learn to keep seeking the next higher plane.

CHAPTER 2

LIFESTYLE

PART I

The loud buzzing of the alarm clock began my usual morning at 5:00, followed by a cup of Starbucks coffee. Since the location I frequented did not open until 6:00, waiting for the doors to open, I spent some time most mornings in the parking lot. Drinking down my cup, a Venti, I would head to the office, where I would then sift through the stacks of papers – uncompleted tasks that littered my desk. Depending on the day and who showed up, I managed a team of six brokers. For most of the morning, I would keep my head down updating spreadsheets or calling vendors. Around 12:00 we would go to lunch, the happy hour of the day. The hour was short, and afterwards, I went back to the office for another six hours of keeping brokers happy, keeping the support staff working toward the end goal, keeping the marketing team on track and accountable, making sure we had the money to pay everyone, and forecasting new projections. Around 6:00 in the evening, we would turn off the lights and leave. But once I got home, my pregnant wife and I would go back out to eat somewhere, finally getting home around 9:30. Trying to read a few pages in a book before going to sleep and hardly eager to get up and do this schedule all over again, I would clutch a book and fight to keep my eyelids open. Repeating this daily routine all week long, I even worked on Saturdays from 8 to 5, as well as on Sunday afternoons. When I say this, I mean it quite literally: I worked *every* day.

This was an outrageous price to pay for such little comfort. Yes, I made a good salary, which meant I could live in a decent house, drive a decent car and even own a boat. What good is a boat you rarely have time to use? Once a year I would take a week-long cram-a-vacation to a cool place with bragging rights, just to go back to work for the other 51 weeks. I was missing something. What was I missing?

I was missing life. I hardly had control of anything. Rather, everything controlled me. Losing my income the same week I was blessed with a child was the best thing that ever happened to me. It was as if God was telling me, *"If you are going to experience the joy of raising a child, I refuse to watch you waste it by working your life away."* After the first year unshackled from the chains of a job, I realized that no amount of money is worth giving up my time. My time is the only thing I truly control, and I need to make sure my money works for me so I don't have to trade my time for money.

That is what Free Me Forever is all about: a way of life. Of course, there is a cost, but it is undeniably worth every penny. To gain this freedom, you have to increase your knowledge, and accordingly, change your habits. Too often, people see these accomplishments as beyond their reach when, in fact, this potential, just waiting to be realized, has been inside you all along. The reward for this process of realization is a better you. Spending your time on self-improvement is one of the most productive things you can possibly do or even imagine.

Changing your thoughts and habits can be difficult, and the beginning can be especially hard. On the surface level, you fight a battle with the world, but on a deeper level, you fight a battle with yourself, your ego which refuses to define you in any other way than by your past. When you change your perspective, you start to see life through the eyes of an independent person. Living becomes much easier and far more satisfying.

PART II

Now, instead of waking up with a set schedule, I wake up with options. If I don't want to do anything, I don't have to. I can't really sketch a "usual day" in my life now, since my days are no longer all the same, but most mornings, depending on when my daughter gets up, I wake up between 6:00 and 7:00. To begin my day, I get my daughter out of bed. Some mornings she hops right up, anxious to go see Mom and little brother; other mornings she wants to read a book or play. I let her dictate the activity, and using my time however I wish, I just enjoy spending these precious moments with her. Once we make it down-stairs, I fix breakfast for the family. On the table, we, trying to eat what is in season locally, always have fresh fruit. Blueberries and straw-berries have been this week's favorite with cantaloupe and watermelon soon to come. My daughter and I picked the blueberries and strawber-ries just last Saturday. The cantaloupe and watermelon came from our local co-op, and every Saturday morning we are in town, we visit the farmer's market for fresh vegetables. I slice all the fruit for everyone in the family, fix the bowls so that the berries are placed just right on top. After we all have our fruit, I help the kids pick out their clothes for the day. Sometimes this can be a drawn-out process, but I don't mind. If my wife and the kids have plans for the day, I help her get packed up and help the kids into the car.

A little later in the morning, around 9:00 or so, I go up the stairs to my home office. After checking my intentions (similar to goals) for the month and year and making any adjustments I need, I usually meditate or study for thirty minutes to an hour, then write or make notes on any plans that come to mind. Around 11:00 I check email, reply to a few, then go out for a run on the beach.

After my run, if it's warm, I go for a swim in the ocean. Most days I meet my business partner John for lunch at a local health food store. Sometimes we plan to go and look at properties later in the afternoon, so I either go with sandy feet and a wet swimsuit, or I go home and shower first. Spending a couple afternoons each week, we look at local proper-ties, and a couple times each month, I travel to look in other cities.

The main difference between my past life and my life now is that, these days, I rarely feel rushed. Instead of feeling like I have to hurry, I feel grateful for life and all that it has provided for me. I now spend time improving myself, loving my family, and quieting my mind. To some of you, this may not sound perfect, but that's fine; you can choose to fill your days any way you like. While I spend time exercising, learning, and being with my family, my business partner John spends his days by perfecting his golf swing or fishing in the Gulf Stream. We both spend a few hours a day thinking about our business, but we can spend that time whenever we want. Usually, we do that over lunch.

One of my favorite things to do is finding new ways to stimulate personal growth, like taking new classes or going to seminars. Just last month, I went to a seminar, and I had dinner with investment bankers and CEOs. The next day I learned how to take a private real estate company public through an IPO (Initial Public Offering). This is not something I see myself doing this year, or even in the near future, but I enjoyed learning the process and meeting the "powerful" people (most of whose daily lives look more like my former rather than my current one). I learned quite a bit, and the knowledge I gained will enable me to speak with authority to my private investors. Of course, I will also pass that knowledge along to my students.

When you gain control of your financial destiny, you gain control of your life. If you depend on someone else for your economic survival, then you end up under his control, just like a kid under the control of a parent. I value my tenants greatly. They get up every morning and work all day to give me 25% to 40% of their paycheck. That money, in turn, pays off the houses where they live. My only risk is that I have to learn how to invest in real estate, while my challenge is that I have to face my fears, buy properties, and get investor funding. I also have to invest my time and money to go to seminars and buy educational materials. In return, my tenants are working for me by paying off my assets with their rent.

CHAPTER 3

MY STORY

So, how did I go from being overworked to being free? Well, I did it step-by-step and piece-by-piece. On the same afternoon I received the call from Bill, I started making calls to friends and past co-workers and explaining the opportunities I could see in the housing market. With the jumbo mortgage market closing and the subprime fallout, I felt like lower-end "workforce" housing was the right market to focus on. I called and explained this to my friend and past-roommate Adam. He happened to live in Charlotte, North Carolina, where I was seeing the most attractive pricing. Also, I knew the Charlotte market was still getting good national press, and some were even calling it the second best market in the country, next to Seattle. But I only got Adam's voicemail: damn! I left a message, trying to spark his interest and explain why his long lost friend was suddenly giving him a ring. It was because I saw a great opportunity! I had seen this all before in the mobile home industry of the late 1990's: the lending got out of line and the foreclosures, called "repos," came streaming back, driving down the prices of mobile homes and driving most dealers out of business. Then, as the dealers went under, the inventory shrank, and prices started to rise. Only a few survivors remained – one of them was Clayton Mobile Homes with Warren Buffett at the wheel.

When Adam didn't answer, I was on to the next call. It was to my friend and business partner John just a few miles from my house. In addition to being friends since high school, we had "invested" together in the past. (I do not consider what we had done in the past investing now, although I did at the time; actually, we were speculating. There is a big difference.) John and I had a relationship at a local bank that I hoped would work for us. *I gave John a call, and as if he had been waiting for my phone call, he was in*! John had been a real estate broker with me in the past at a small company so we were familiar with one another's thinking on real estate and investing. Also, we had both been burned by the nasty market turn. I had my problem property, and so did he. Both of us depended on real estate to make a living, and we both had large interest payments to make. What better common urgency and motivation!

Next, I called another high school friend Ed, a realtor in the Charlotte area who had sold homes in many of the neighborhoods where I was looking. He didn't seem to want to work together, but he offered to show me around and tell me what he knew. Ed also knew about HUD foreclosures, which ended up offering a great source of inventory.

Then I called Steve, who worked at a bank in Winston-Salem, a small city in North Carolina made famous by Camel cigarettes. Spelling out my past experience in the mobile home business, as well as the discovery of houses for $.50 on the dollar, I told him about my plan. I informed him about the jumbo loan meltdown and the subprime fallout and told him this was my chance to create a fortune! Steve then told me that, as the branch manager of the bank, he had the authority to loan up to $100,000 without having to go to anyone else. *I was in. He would put up my first $100,000!*

Next, I called my bank to see if I could get the equity line on my primary residence extended. I had opened the equity line when buying the home, but with the down payment amount for the house, it was tapped out. The banker said he would have to order a new appraisal. He took down my phone number and said that an appraiser would call me over the next few days to set up the on-site inspection. I wanted to up the equity-line by $100,000, so I needed my house to appraise for at least $435,000. With the jumbo mortgage market frozen, I knew property values in the jumbo category were going to drop, so time was of the essence. I knew I had to refinance, and it was now or never. I started pulling comps for the appraiser to justify the price I wanted.

Meanwhile, by the next Monday, Adam emailed me back and said he had some interest, even though at the time, our thoughts on investing were pretty far apart. Once again: *I was in!* On September 22, 2007, just seven days after I had received the life changing phone call, I emailed an outline of a business plan and strategy. A few days later, we had attorneys drawing up the corporate documents.

In my first few days of freedom, I had found a partner in Adam, and we started to focus on the market I believed had the most potential because of prices and availability of funds. Shortly thereafter, we started our company. Having been friends since high school and having lived together through most of college, we knew each other quite well, but we had never before invested together. We both came from working class families, and having made all of our money on our own, I knew we would probably do well as business partners. Adam brought several strengths to the team. One, he had a pretty high income. Two, he could help with website and marketing materials. Three, he had remodeled several homes with his unbelievable artistic ability. Making the home look nice and overseeing contractors, Adam enjoys the "field work" of asset management while I enjoy putting together the spreadsheets, talking with bankers, and managing the books on the business end.

I had also rekindled my work relationship with John. In the past, John and I had formed a company. We put it together as a single purpose LLC, to buy a house back from a guy to whom we had brokered a house. He had gotten into some financial trouble, and having bought him out, we sold it to another investor for a $30k profit. When we were brokers, we had flipped some property and made quick profits, however, at this point, we both had our minds on more conservative plays. We wanted properties that would produce long-term cash flow. We were done with the risky, speculative stuff of our past. As I mentioned earlier, we both carried large interest payments from bad "investments" that we had discovered to be merely speculations. John has a high net worth and ample real estate experience. Also, we had a banking relationship to try to reestablish, so we went to work. The down side of working with John was that we both derived our income from real estate, which, when the sky is falling, banks tend to dislike. By putting aside any doubts, we set an appointment to go see our banker from the past. With great reluctance and after being tossed from banker to banker, we were able to get a commitment for three rentals. Of course, this was not easy, and the lenders did not say "yes" the first time. As a matter of fact, they refused to give us the final "yes" until we took in two houses that we had put under contract at the same time. When the appraisal for the first one came back at $95,000, and we had it under contract for $35,000, the lenders agreed to give us the other one. We had put up our earnest money without knowing where the purchase money was going to come from, but we knew we had to find it somewhere, and what better motivation than the pressure of losing money! John and I continue to put ourselves under pressure like this even today. Have we lost some earnest money? Sure. Have we made more than we have lost? Lots more!

After talking some more with Steve, the branch manager from Winston-Salem, I found that he could only authorize 85% of the purchase price of the house, but if I bought the house with cash, he could do a "cash-out, refinance" at 85% of the appraisal or tax value. This means I could buy a house for $100,000 with a bank loan and get $85,000, requiring $15,000 of my own money to seal the deal, or I could buy the home with cash, and if the tax value was at least $118,000, I could refinance it and put the entire $100,000 back in my pocket. I needed cash! I needed that equity line!

A few days later, the appraiser called to set up the appointment for my personal residence. Now, from my years in the real estate business, I know what an appraiser can and cannot value in a home, but I also know from my experience as salesperson, as well as a student of psychology, how you can influence someone's thinking subconsciously. My wife and I cleaned the house, as clean as possible. I bought fresh flowers for all the tables. When the appraiser arrived, we had vegetable soup cooking on the stove and cookies baking in the oven. Meanwhile, classical music played in the background. The key is to please all the five senses!

I had handpicked the comparable sales I thought would show the home in the best light. They were a stretch because the homes and the neighborhood I had picked as comps were newer, and to be perfectly honest, nicer than my house, but not so much nicer that it was obvious. He was definitely going to have to want to make the appraisal for me emotionally because there were other comps in more similar neighborhoods that would not justify the value I wanted and needed. As we walked around the house, I made sure to mention my situation: I had a newborn baby, and I needed the money for a new business venture. I know it probably didn't matter to the appraiser, but I thought he should know that I was going to use the money to better my life, not to buy a new TV.

Then, a little bit of magic happened; something I didn't even realize until weeks later, when we got the appraisal back in the mail from the onsite inspection. As the appraiser went up to do the inspection on the top floor of the house, my daughter, just a few weeks old, started crying hysterically. My wife, trying to quiet her down, ducked into the nursery to breast-feed her. She didn't want the appraiser to be upset by a crying baby, and before the appraiser arrived, we had talked about how to make the visit as pleasant as possible. The appraiser then inspected all the other rooms, and turning to me, said he would have to inspect the nursery in order to get every room in the house. I answered, "Sure, I understand," and slowly opened the door. There sat my wife breastfeeding my daughter. Needless to say, the appraiser did not spend much time looking around that room. As a matter of fact, he quickly pulled the door shut and said he had what he needed. I walked him to the door, handed him my comp sheets, and chatted with him the best I could, without seeming overbearing or too obvious.

When the loan specialist called and said our appraisal came back at $460,000, I was overjoyed! Wow! I wondered how that could happen, but of course, did not ask. Then the woman on the phone asked: "Would you like to up the amount of your credit-line request Mr. Harper?" I responded, "Sure."

It was not until we received our copy of the appraisal in the mail that I realized what had happened. The room we were using as a nursery was really an office or study, and without a closet, could not be considered a bedroom for the appraisal. But because my wife had startled the appraiser with her breastfeeding, he failed to notice that the room lacked a closet, counted the room as a bedroom, and we scored a more direct comparison to the higher comps I had showed him, in turn giving us the higher value. My newborn daughter had done her part to get us the highest value possible!

A few days later, I traveled to Charlotte to look at more houses. Adam and I were concentrating on that area; John and I were looking anywhere we could to get money and cash flowing properties, and I was looking for a solid cash flow property with a high tax value. I had gone from no job and no prospects to trying to find properties for three companies in a very short time. Although funding was still an issue, I was in the hunt. I found my first serious subject property in Mt. Holly outside of Charlotte. Originally asking $99,000, the banker dropped the price to $70,000 the day I made the offer because of all the work it needed. I gave the reduced asking price, cash with a two week closing. The agent called back and said he had two other offers, but because mine was cash, the bank had accepted. Two weeks later, I owned my first rental property after paying for it with cash from my newly created equity line. A few days after that, I was refinancing it with Steve for $100,000. I got the $70,000 I had paid from my newly created equity line, plus money for repairs and a little to spare. With a whole lot of luck and divine intervention, I was finally in business. That was just the beginning!

Looking back at those first few steps that I took to get started, it is obvious that a few things made a huge difference in my success. Many of them are outlined in a book called *Think and Grow Rich* by Napoleon Hill. I first bought it during the Christmas season of 2006, and since then, I've read it at least three times. If you are serious about success, you must read this timeless classic.

First, I had a burning desire. With a newborn daughter to provide for and a wife who had just quit her job, the last thing I wanted to do was tell my wife she had to go back to work. We had it all planned out. We would have kids, cut back on spending, and she would be able to stay home and take care of them. All couples decide for themselves what lifestyles work best, but for us, this was very important. We didn't want to miss our daughter growing up, just so we could make more money or be more "comfortable." That would have seemed like such a waste: to miss a once in a lifetime experience just to be able to drive a better car or live in a slightly bigger house. We had committed to rearing our own children, and I was absolutely not going to let my wife down. I was committed, and I was going to fulfill my burning desire.

I also had a burning desire to get out of the daily grind. I had tried working for other people, and I could see it didn't work for me. If you work for someone else, they have control over your life. I couldn't think of a more pitiful way to exist. Just think of having to wake up every day with concerns about pleasing other people. I wanted options!

Second, I had faith. Even though I was up against unbelievable odds (very little money, no job, banks failing), I set out on a course that I felt was the best for me in the long run. The fact of the matter was that I did not have any idea how I was going to get money to buy rental houses, nor did I have any clue how buying rental houses was going to help me cover the $3500 a month payment I had to make on my speculative house; I did know, however, that I had finished speculating, and that the only true way to invest in real estate was to buy income producing property. I did know that I wanted to be an investor and not trade my time for money. Acknowledging these truths, I sat out to execute my plan. I had faith that if I took the correct steps, things would work to my advantage. I had faith that if I did what my heart told me was right, things would work out, even if my brain didn't quite grasp everything all at once.

Third, I made a decision and took action. I didn't wait until I had all the facts. I didn't wait until I knew the market was at the bottom, which it wasn't and might not be currently. Using all the information I had, I evaluated the situation the best I could at the present time, and I moved forward. I called everyone I knew that might be interested in helping me. I called everyone I knew that might be interested in helping themselves. I made a list of every way I could get money to fund my deals. I made lists of all the people I knew, or knew of, who might be able to help me, and I picked up the phone and started calling with no further delay.

I acted in the face of fear. Of course I was afraid, but I didn't let fear immobilize me. Instead, I used it as a catalyst. I used the fear to help me proceed quickly but cautiously. Everyone has a fear of failing, but I had an even greater fear: letting my family down. And most of all, I didn't want to let myself down. I knew I could do anything I wanted, if I gave it all that I had. If I used my knowledge, made a plan, executed the plan in spite of fear without procrastination, and adjusted the plan as I went along when new information became available to me, I would succeed. You can do the same thing.

CHAPTER 4

INVESTING VS. SPECULATING

Have you ever imagined what it would be like to be an investor? To be someone who makes all his money by using his knowledge and ideas instead of trading his time for money. To be someone who has unlimited earning potential. To be someone who has passive income flowing into his life every day regardless of where he is, whom he is with, or what he is doing. Do you want to be able to spend your time doing exactly what you want?

Most people don't allow themselves the freedom to think these thoughts. Most people think it is simply out of reach and don't want to go through the disappointment of brainstorming about the possibilities of an unlimited life. A life where you control your time, and it is not traded every day for money. A life where you make all the decisions. A life where you are only limited by your imagination. I want to challenge you to change this mind-set today. I want to challenge you to take control of your life by taking control of your mind and erasing your fears. Fear is really the only thing holding us back. Fear is the only thing that keeps us from reaching our true potential. Fear is what keeps us trading our time for money instead of using our knowledge to create unlimited wealth!

I think that most of you probably feel like you need to go to work every day to support your family and loved ones. I know I did. I also know how helpless I felt when I was holding my four day old daughter with no money coming into my life as of that day. Here she was depending on me for her very existence, and I didn't have a clue how I was going to support her. That day I vowed to never let that happen again. I vowed to never again place my financial well being in someone else's hands. I vowed from that day on to learn to be an investor, to put my personal finances first, to take them into my own hands and not spend one more second of my time on making someone else wealthy.

Do you spend most of your time working to make yourself wealthy or working to make other people wealthy? Most of us don't think of it this way, but it is exactly what we do. We get up and go to work every day and spend forty hours a week focused on making someone else wealthy. It could be your boss, the owner of the company or even the stock holders of the company, the company's investors. Do you get up every morning and focus on making them money all day every day while you come home and ignore your own financial situation? You ignore the fact that you hand over a percentage of your paycheck to a financial planner whom you know very little about and who possibly knows even less about you. You ignore the fact that you have no clue whether the amount you are giving that person is really going to be enough for you to retire on. You ignore the fact that you really have no clue where your money is being invested. You simply hand your money over to someone who you hope is more qualified than you and pray the market does not go down.

I was lucky. My job was taken away, my paycheck was taken away, and my profession was in the middle of a crisis. I had no choice but to come up with a new way of thinking. I had no choice but to acquire knowledge quickly so that I could move my life in the direction I wanted to go. Those of you who have a job right now have it the hardest. You have to convince yourself that it is worth the extra effort to take your financial freedom into your own hands without the motivation of fear and pain that some people are experiencing. It will be easier if you think of the time that you are trading for money. Some of you are a slave to money, and you are the same people that say you don't care about money. You might say that money is not important to you, yet you spend one half of all your awake hours trading your most precious asset, time, for money. Time is by far our biggest and most precious asset. Once a moment in your life is gone, it is gone forever. You can never get it back. You can't save time, you can only spend it. The moment that you are experiencing right now is true life. Everything else is a fantasy. If you spend your time wishing away the present by dreaming about the future, I can think of no sadder situation to experience.

The good news is that anyone can change. Everyone can change. That is what makes us human. We can realize what we are doing, reflect on it and change it!

Now that I was unemployed, I knew that I needed to educate myself on being an investor. I realized that working for other people was not working; I reflected on that fact and made the decision to not continue down that path. It was time for a change.

As I set out to become an investor, my first stop was the bookstore. My first purchase was a few books on Warren Buffet. Who better to learn from? Although he does not invest in real estate, I quickly learned that his investment principles could be applied perfectly. I also realized that I had been in real estate for over twelve years and had never really read many books on investing in real estate. I chose a few to read.

As I began reading, I learned two very important things. First, most books written on investing in real estate were not very good. Second, Warren Buffett had a teacher named Benjamin Graham whom he credits with giving him the foundation he built his investment empire on. I found out that Benjamin Graham wrote a book called *The Intelligent Investor* and that Warren Buffett said it's "by far the best book on investing ever written." I was sold. I purchased it and started reading.

In *The Intelligent Investor*, Graham analyzes the difference between speculation and investing. This is a key concept to being a successful investor, a concept that I had not previously grasped. When I had "invested" in the $1.2 million dollar "spec" home, I did not realize that there was no investing involved. It was pure speculation. That is why it is called a "spec" home. You would think that someone who had been a real estate broker for twelve years would have understood this concept, but I did not. I could be the only one, but my fear is that I am not alone.

So what is the difference between investing and speculating? In its simplest form, speculating is buying something with the hope that the price will go up. Investing, on the other hand, is an activity that "promises safety of principal and an adequate return." Let me explain this in real estate terms.

I lost a significant amount of money on the speculative home that I had built with the other partners. Let's examine why. First, you must realize as *The Intelligent Investor* explains, that you cannot control the market, and it is very hard, if not impossible, to predict what the market is going to do. The market has a psychology behind it. That psychology is the group psychology of the participating investors and speculators. After we built the house that had originally appraised for $1,250,000, the market turned quickly. First, there was the jumbo loan crisis along with the subprime crash. This triggered more inventory to hit the market as everyone, all of a sudden, wanted out. This pushed prices down further and further as more inventory kept hitting the market with fewer and fewer buyers.

Back to the first question, why did we lose money? Did the market cause us to lose money? My feeling is no. It was our investment, or more accurately labeled, speculator strategy. You only lose money when you sell. The reason we lost money was because we sold. Why did we sell? We were losing around $7000 a month in interest payments we were making on a house that was worth less and less every day. Was this the right thing to do? Considering our circumstance, it was our only choice. We looked into renting the home, but the most we could get in rent was $4000 with most people quoting more like $2100. We just couldn't lock ourselves into a contract where we were losing $3000 or more every month.

But let's look at this from the beginning again. What if we had purchased 24 houses for $50,000 each and rented those out for $800 a month? Let's say our payments on the homes are $300 a month and property taxes and insurance are $200 a month. Now let's assume that the market took a plunge, and the value of these houses dropped the same. Would you lose money? No. Why would you even think about selling? You are making $7200 in cash flow every month after paying your payments, taxes and insurance. You would never think about selling something for a loss that is paying you money, especially $7200 a month. It doesn't matter what the market is doing. You are still making money.

This is the difference. The first case study is speculation, because if the market does not cooperate, you don't make money, and as you have seen from this example, you can lose a lot of money. The second proposed scenario, which is what I did from that day forward, is investing. You are protecting your principal and ensuring an adequate return on your money. So here is the Million dollar secret to investing in real estate: You must invest in income producing properties that have cash flow. To do anything else is pure speculation. To speculate is to gamble. Can you make a lot of money speculating? Absolutely! Can you lose a lot? Yes, I know from experience. Choose investing!

CHAPTER 5

ANALYZING THE MARKET

After stressing out for most of the afternoon and fretting about what I was going to do, I decided to go back to my roots. Before Summer Creek, the development where I had recently been working, I had been an average Realtor selling average houses, mostly foreclosures, to ordinary people who worked ordinary jobs. This was before the market went crazy, and everyone wanted a million dollar house. Seeing what the market was doing, I decided I would return to my days of helping the working class person. It didn't take long to get tired of hearing people complain about the high prices of lots on the waterway or dealing with people wanting to know all the details with very little intention of actually moving into the neighborhood. I longed for dealing with people who needed homes – people who didn't have enough time to waste mine. I decided to check out the foreclosure market.

One of the first places I looked was the HUD and VA foreclosure sites, which listed homes throughout the country. I had learned about them at the beginning of my career; while taking some "time off" from college, I worked for a small real estate company that specialized in selling these houses. Although I had only worked there a short time, sold nothing, and partied more than I worked, I did remember one thing: the advantage to selling these homes, especially for HUD, is they pay a 5% commission to the buyer's agent. This is 2% to 3% higher than you can get from most sellers.

Looking around at these foreclosure sites, I started brainstorming ways to market and sell these homes. Hoping to move out of the Wilmington market that was leaving me so badly burned, I began to look at different markets. I noticed that apparently new houses – most of which had been built in the 2004, 2005, and 2006 ranges – were selling for $50 to $60k. Naturally, this piqued my interest.

At this same time, I had started to read *The Intelligent Investor* by Benjamin Graham. Thinking back to what I had been reading while looking at the number and price of all these foreclosed homes, I realized now is not the time to sell real estate, but now is the time to buy real estate. Why go against the market and try to sell homes at a time when the general public is scared to buy? You have to swim *with* the current, right? Not against it. If the market wants to give me homes at a discount, I decided, I would take them. Since there was nothing in my local area to match the low prices I was seeing in Charlotte, I decided on seeking out the low-priced homes. Also, as I found out, the local market in Charlotte was still doing well overall. The media was calling it the hottest market in the country, competing for the top spot with Seattle; yet, I was seeing homes selling for $60k that had recently sold for $125k. I had to go take a look for myself. There was only one problem: I had a 3 week old daughter.

My college roommate Adam, whom I was hoping to recruit as a business partner, spent the next two days riding with me around Charlotte and looking at all the foreclosures I had pulled off the internet. What we found was mind boggling. We would ride into neighborhoods, new neighborhoods with row after row of boarded up houses. These were not old run-down places like you see boarded up in every city. These houses were brand new, recently built neighborhoods that had instantly become ghettos. From neighborhood to neighborhood, we rode around that first day just trying to figure out what in the hell was going on. Seeing it mostly on the West, North, and East side of the city, we started charting the areas by placing dots on a map of the city. Then our chart revealed something strange. All these neighborhoods were an equal distance from the center of the city, just like a ring around Saturn. After looking at neighborhood after neighborhood, we headed back to Adam's house in a revitalized section right outside of downtown Charlotte. It took us a while to understand what we had seen that day. How had this happened?

That evening, thinking hard about many things, I reflected on what I had seen. First, I thought about how it was such a shame that these new houses were boarded up, some covered with graffiti. Then I thought about how we were sitting in a restored neighborhood of 1920's and 30's bungalows that, just a few years earlier, had been a drug and crime infested war zone. Now there were new moms driving Range Rovers. How might the two be connected? The new vinyl ghettos of suburbia had drawn the criminals out of the inner city neighborhood that was being revived. Then I remembered when I had seen something very similar to this happen before.

The mobile home industry of the late 1990's was an exact foreshadowing of the subprime bust of 2007. Anyone who was involved or followed that industry should have known exactly what was going to happen. I had worked during the mobile home industries' subprime disaster on the front lines as a sales person. Selling double-wide mobile homes to people for $0 down, I had started to work for a fortune 1000 company that soon went bankrupt. The buyers would just walk on the sales lot, sign their names, and we would deliver their new home with a payment book to send checks in the mail. No money needed. Then, as a sales person, I would collect a $4000 commission check. I made over $14,000 in my first four weeks on the job! Having only graduated from college a month earlier, I made over $75,000 during my first year. It seemed too good to be true, and it was. As repos mounted (repo is short for repossession and is the same thing as a foreclosure, but mobile homes are thought of as more like cars), everything came crashing down. Soon the company went bankrupt, and I found myself selling repos for the banks. One thing I had learned from that experience that I could apply to my current situation: when the repos came back in numbers, it pushed the prices on mobile homes way down, and many, even *most* mobile home dealerships went out of business. When they all went out of business, they stopped building homes. When they stopped building homes, supplies dropped, and then prices went right back up. Maybe not to where they were before, but they recovered nicely; Warren Buffett's Berkshire Hathaway is one of the largest shareholders of one of the few companies that is left.

Knowing this, I decided to buy some of these homes, rent them out, and see if the market recovered. I decided to continue my search.

I didn't know this at the time, but real estate follows a market cycle. Once you understand the market cycle, you can look at any market in the country, or the world for that matter, and identify the current stage of the cycle, enabling you to use the correct strategy for making money. This is the main difference between sophisticated investors and amateurs. Sophisticated investors can make money in any market, whether it is rising or falling; amateurs do well when the market is going up but get clobbered when the market turns.

Since real estate is a cyclical business, as you know, you have to ride the cycles. In your local market, you must identify the current phase in the market cycle then alter your investment strategy to match the current and future cyclical phases. Also, there are always markets rising throughout the country. These markets are doing well, no matter what the national trends are doing or the national press is saying. Here are the four phases of the real estate market: recession, recovery, expansion and oversupply.

Recession

In this cycle, demand is low and supplies are high. Prices and rents are falling and vacancies are increasing. Unemployment is at its highest. Time on the market is the longest. There is no speculation. Existing inventory is sitting idle. Foreclosures sharply increase. Construction is overpriced and stagnant. Investment properties are priced at the lowest levels. Typically, local government has to do something to turn the things around and bring jobs to the area.

Your investment strategy in the Recession: The bottom is falling out of the market, and no one knows where the bottom is or when it will hit. Prices are falling, rents are falling, and people are panicking. You can find excellent deals if you are confident enough to act and able to handle prices possibly dropping below your purchase price. You want to buy well located properties with significant cash flow. With cash flow in place, you can ride the wave.

Recovery

The Multi-Millionaire Maker! In this phase, time on the market decreases. Demand begins to increase, and absorbs oversupply. Job growth increases. Prices slowly increase. Rents slowly increase as vacancies decrease. There is very little speculation. Existing properties are being rehabbed. Foreclosure competition is fierce as numbers decline.

Your investment strategy in Recovery: Buy, Buy, Buy! Buy everything you can get your hands on as long as cash flow covers your expenses. You can pay market price because today's prices are tomorrow's bargains. Rents are expected to rise as vacancy rates compress, so you can buy on a slightly positive cash flow. Find all the financing and partners you can. This is the multi-millionaire maker.

Expansion

In this phase, supplies are low and demand starts rising. Foreclosures decrease in number to almost zero Properties sell fast. Employment is higher. Prices and rent are rising fast. Speculation is in full swing. Construction starts to accelerate. You start to see homes being torn down and properties changed to the highest and best use. DEMAND IS AT ITS HIGHEST!

Your Strategy? Buy and hold, until you see the market entering Over Supply. Buying in the middle of the cycle, you have to be cautious. It would have been better to have bought in Recovery, but you can still make money, just make sure you don't hold your purchases too long. Make sure the properties you buy offer steady cash flow!

Oversupply

In this final stage before the cycle repeats, time on the market increases. The number of properties increase. Rents become stagnant. People are still getting inflated prices. The potential for overbuilding increases. Investment properties are bought on speculation, not cash flow (but not by you, of course!) Demand for construction and materials are still rising. Foreclosures remain slow but steady. Businesses begin to slow, and job creation slows.

Your Strategy: Sell, Sell, Sell. Once you recognize that your market has gone into Oversupply, you need to sell immediately. Inventory will increase as everyone tries to cash out. If you miss the turn, then you could be holding your property for a long time, as much as ten years. The key indicators to watch will be the days on the market, or DOM, and vacancy rates. The DOM and vacancy rates will increase before prices correct giving you ample time to cash out. This is one of the most important points in the entire book. When you see DOM and vacancies increase, cut your price to below market and sell everything in your portfolio! Get in a cash position so you can pick up the pieces after the fall and ride the wave again.

Now, as most of you know, some markets are in the Recession right now. However, some markets have emerged into Recovery, and others are fast approaching the Recovery. I don't know how much you know about surfing, but investing in real estate is a lot like surfing. When you surf, can you wait until the wave is under you to start paddling? No. If you do, you will miss the wave. You can't start paddling when the wave gets to you, you have to anticipate the wave and get ready. You have to sit up on your board and look out at the ocean to see the waves coming. Once you see them on the way, you have to point your board toward the beach and start to build momentum by paddling. You look back over your shoulder to make sure the wave is still there and that you are in position, but you are paddling and building momentum. You have to be ready for the wave when it hits. Then the wave suddenly whisks you toward the beach with no effort at all.

If you watch amateurs learning to surf, they wait until the wave is on them and paddle as fast as they can as the wave passes them by. They end up tired and frustrated, scratching their heads behind the wave. The pros, on the other hand, see the wave coming. They make a few quick strokes to get in position before the wave arrives. And when it does, it sweeps them away with oceanic might.

So imagine yourself surfing currents of the real estate cycle. You can't start investing when the wave gets here, or you will miss it. You have to anticipate then act at the right moment to build up momentum.

Get your team in place. Get your position with your board pointed toward the beach. Then when the wave comes, you can ride it with very little effort, while everyone who did not prepare paddles as fast as he can, wearing himself out, only to get left behind.

Don't miss the wave! Stay informed. Anticipate market moves. Network and learn from professionals who know how to get awesome results with very little effort. Don't end up tired and frustrated looking at the back of a wave you should be riding.

CHAPTER 6

PRIVATE MONEY

I know a question on everyone's mind: how do I raise private money? It's a vital question. The ability to raise money proves essential to any entrepreneur, or even for that matter, any CEO. The top executive of a company, regardless of industry or size, must understand that the primary goal is to raise money. In real estate, our ability to raise money dictates the projects we can do, how fast we can do them, and how freely we live our lives along the way. The ability to raise private money opens up tremendous opportunity and will make you wealthy much quicker than relying on banks or other traditional channels of funding.

Before we start our discussion of the different types of money you can raise, we should clearly understand how money comes to us from more traditional sources. For many years, at the single-family level, banks have provided the main source of real estate funding. A bank simply takes the depositor's money, pays a low interest rate, then lends those funds to a borrower at a higher interest rate. Banks, therefore, make their money on the interest rate spread. So, over-simplified for clarity, your aunt Edna deposits her savings into the bank on the corner, receiving around 2% or so in today's market. The bank then turns around and loans you the money to buy a foreclosure at 7% interest. This way, the bank makes 5% interest off Aunt Edna's money. The bank makes its money at the expense of both Aunt Edna and you. Alternatively, Aunt Edna can lend her money directly to you at 6%, making 4% more than she will in the bank, and you can lower your interest expense by 1%, thus making more profit.

Now before we move forward, let's take a step back for an overview of the types of private money we can raise. Basically, there are two kinds: debt and equity. Debt is money that you borrow and must pay back. Equity is money that an investor gives you for a portion of ownership in the deal in anticipation of a share of future profit. Since debt is the easiest to explain to friends and family, who might be a little adverse to risk, let's focus first on it.

Debt is usually borrowed for a fixed rate of return. For instance, you may borrow $100,000 from Aunt Edna at 6% annual interest with a balloon in 36 months. During the term of the loan, you may make interest-only payments. These terms are easy for everyone to understand and can be calculated quickly. Let me explain. First, the terms: the loan covers a term of 36 months, and the deal requires you to pay the loan back in full at the end of those three years. If you are tying this note to a specific property with a deed of trust, then the note will be due upon the sale of the property or on the three-year deadline whichever comes first. Since the payments are interest only, you will have the entire balance due, $100,000. Also, since the payments are interest only, you can figure out the payments without an amortization schedule. (However, if you email me at kyle@freemeforever.com and insert "amortization table" in the title line then I will email you a spreadsheet.) When you multiply the $100,000 loan amount by the 6% annual interest rate, you get an annual interest payment of $6000. Of course, you can set up your payment terms however you want, as long as you both agree. Nothing says you have to make payments every month. Regardless of what most people think, that is just what the banks have trained us to think. Most of the time, when I borrow private money in the form of debt, I negotiate to make my payments quarterly. This way I avoid the hassle of processing a payment every month. So, if you and Aunt Edna agreed on quarterly payments, then you will make four installments of $1500 once every three months. As you can see, Aunt Edna already gives you more flexibility than a bank.

Another option, especially if you were going to do a one-year lease purchase for your buyer/tenant – one of my favorite strategies – would be to make the payment annually. This allows you to pay installments with principal repayment upon the sale of the property, meanwhile giving you an exceptionally nice cash flow. Of course, getting all your dates lined up perfectly takes careful planning, but already you can see how private debt offers you greater power and freedom. Thus the beauty of private debt: the structures are only limited by your level of creativity.

I raised my first private money in the form of debt. This is probably the easiest to explain to people who are new to business structure and real estate investing. I raised $70,000 for repairs and other miscellaneous business expenses when I purchased a property in January of 2009. For quite some time, I had been talking to the investor who had money in CDs and was having to search and search to get a minimal return when one came due. On several occasions, he had questioned me about what I was doing in real estate. Giving him my overall plan, I told him the details about the homes I had purchased. I talked about how, once the repairs were complete, the homes offered equity instantly. I told him I could take a home with a tax value of $129,000, purchase it for $80,000 because it needed repairs, then upon completing the repairs (such as carpet and paint for $10,000), the house would be worth $134,900. I told him we could attach the debt directly to the house with a deed of trust; therefore, if anything completely unexpected were to happen, he could claim the house as collateral and recover his principal. For instance, if he loaned me the $90,000 to purchase and fix up the house, and I could not rent or sell it, he could foreclose on the home and take it as collateral. Of course, I assured him that this was only a worst case scenario; as most homes, I told him, could be rented quickly for cash flow to cover the interest payments. With an investor like him, it's supremely important to make sure he knows that, regardless of what happens, he can recover his money.

Remember: debt investors will avoid risk. They will only loan money for a fixed rate of return. When I raised my first money back in January of 2009, we used a promissory note as the legal instrument. In raising debt, most likely, you will do the same. In my case, the investor was comfortable with me personally, so we made the deal without a deed of trust. This gave me the option of using the money on several different projects, or to combine the money with bank money, in order to leverage it for a higher return. For instance, I could use $20,000 of the private debt as a down payment and purchasing a house for $100,000, then get a bank loan for 80% of the purchase price, or $80,000. This way, I work the deal without using any of my own money, and from my perspective, that means 100% financing. From the bank's perspective, it is 80% financing, which meets the underwriting standards for a loan at most banks. This is one way to achieve $0 down investing.

Loan structure can also be negotiated with a private lender. When you go to the bank for a loan, the banker typically wants you to put down a certain percentage of the purchase price. Usually he will only finance 80% or so, and if you need to complete repairs, then he only loans you 80% toward those as well. If the repairs prove significant enough, he will require you set up a draw schedule, so that you will get the money in installments when certain, bank-approved repairs are complete. Usually, the banker will have to come to the property to inspect what you have completed prior to releasing the money. All of this takes time and involves paperwork. Further, the banker will make you get an appraisal, probably a "subject to" appraisal; that is, an appraisal of the property subject to the completion of repairs. In other words, the appraisal includes the finished product with the repairs.

Now let's think about the same loan as private debt. Let's say you plan to buy a house for $80,000. You need to replace the carpet, paint both the interior and exterior, and replace the roof, at an estimated cost of $15,000. The tax value on the home is $129,900, and based on comparable sales in the neighborhood (information provided by our Realtor), you think you can do a lease/purchase on the home and sell it at the end of the one-year lease period for $134,900. With a $1000 earnest money check from our personal funds, not knowing exactly where you are going to get the money, you put the home under contract. Maybe you have already talked to Aunt Edna about your real estate investing, and asking you to give her a call when we see another opportunity, she has shown interest. We call her and tell her we've found a house that looks fantastic.

You show her the house and tell her about our plans for repairs. You show her the comparable sales and rentals in the neighborhood along with our cash flow analysis of the property, which you created with the free software you received from emailing me. Then you show her the contract price plus the repair estimates and ask her for a loan for the entire purchase and repair price of $95,000, plus $5000 to cover closing costs and other miscellaneous expenses. Feeling comfortable with our plans and figures, she agrees to loan us the money.

To get a jump on marketing with the permission of the seller, you have your agent put a for sale/lease sign in the yard. You also go ahead and have our Realtor list the property on the MLS, subject to you taking title to the property. Because this was such a find, you show the house right away and meet a young couple who really want to live in this neighborhood. Some of the few buyers with imagination, the couple can envision the home after repairs. So they make an offer with their agent for the full price, but they ask for a reduced rent during the lease period of 12 months. The reason they want a lease purchase is to help them pay down some credit card debt, bringing into balance their debt-to-income ratio. They have been working with their mortgage broker to accomplish this, and they only have a few more things to pay down. Our broker asks theirs to provide a written statement proving this is true, and we receive verification.

Now you decide to go back to Aunt Edna. The buyers, the Joneses, have said they can only pay $500 a month while they pay down their debt before the option period ends in one year. You discuss this with Aunt Edna, telling her that we would like to have one year and a month before having the first payment due. When you show her the contract along with the approval letter from the mortgage broker, she agrees to give us the loan, with an annual payment of $6000 and a 30-day grace period before the payment is considered late. This gives you the time to complete the repairs in the first 30 days, so the buyers can move in with a year lease and a purchase date of one year from move-in. Also, we require a nonrefundable option fee of $5000 from the sellers at the time that they sign the lease/option, a $500 deposit, and $500 for the first month's rent. You document the $5000 you receive by making a copy of the check for the nonrefundable option fee and deposit it into our business bank account to create a paper trail. You know the mortgage broker will need a copy to give credit for the money the buyers gave us toward their down payment.

We tell Aunt Edna you plan to close in two weeks and ask her to have the money ready by then. She says it's no problem. Next you call the attorney handling the close for your purchase and ask the attorney to keep you on the books for the original closing date, but also whether she has an open time slot to pencil us in for Friday, just two weeks away. You tell her our funding source has committed to that day, but knowing how things go, you want to keep the original date in case the funds don't arrive. Sure enough, on the Thursday before the close, Aunt Edna calls and says the bank can't get the funds into her checking account until Monday. Now it's your turn to tell her no problem, since we can change the closing, and you call the attorney to confirm the original closing date. Aunt Edna ends up getting the funds over to the attorney's office the next Thursday. Since you still have a week before the original closing date, this works perfectly.

Purchasing the home, you walk away from closing with a check for $17,237. Now you have our $15,000 for repairs, plus a little extra from the closing costs you didn't need to pay the attorney; you pay the homeowners insurance (which has Aunt Edna listed as a beneficiary) and pay the prorated property taxes. The contactors go to work on the home immediately. Our buyers are set to sign the lease purchase at our attorney's office on the 31st, so you tell the contractors the move-in date is the 21st to assure enough time for the completion of repairs.

The contractors are finishing up the final touches when the buyers arrive to move in on the 31st. You have just deposited the $5000 option fee in your account, along with the $500 rent check, and you have turned the $500 security deposit over to a property management company to place in an Escrow account. As is typical, your repairs went $2000 over budget, but luckily you had the extra funds from closing. Now you have made $5500 off the property, which we put in our business's operating account, in case it's needed. You have taken no money out of pocket, and you now have $5500 in the bank, all from using our real estate knowledge!

Equity

If you think private debt opens up doors and options for real estate investing, just wait until you see how far equity can take you toward freedom. Equity is cash. It is usually cash paid in exchange for ownership in the company that is going to invest. There are two main ways that I have used equity to fund deals. First is another investor and you start a company where you are partners or you both manage the company. Second and my personal favorite is when you sell shares or units of your company to raise capital. The first can be very effective. The second is when you are heading for the big time!

Let's start by going through an example of you starting a form of partnership with another investor. For instance, you decide that you are going to start looking around for some real estate to invest in, so you create an LLC. You come up with a name that you would like, and you search the Secretary of State website and find that there is another company with the same name you wanted. You go back to the drawing board. You then decide that your street name Greenville combined with Capital would make a good name. You search for Greenville Capital, and it appears to be available. You then fill out the paperwork that you find online to set up the LLC. You mail out your initial paper work along with your check for the starting fees. When you receive your package back from the Secretary of State, you go to the IRS website and apply for a federal tax id number. You can now use this number to open up a bank account for your new company, Greenville Capital, LLC. Next you read a few books, go to a seminar on investing in income producing properties and start looking at the foreclosed properties in your neighborhood.

At one of the seminars you attend, you meet Phil. Phil happens to be from your same home town, and you discuss how ironic it is that you fly across the country to meet each other. Phil is also interested in buying income producing property to create a retirement fund for himself. He currently works as an engineer for a large Fortune 500 company, but he understands that his 401k will probably not provide for all of his needs and wants to diversify in real estate. He has read many of the same books you have, and you both agree that you want to buy lower end houses that have cash flow from rental income. You tell Phil that you have been looking at several homes in your market that meet this requirement and that you already have a company set up to purchase the homes.

You then admit that the only thing that has kept you from making an offer on a few of them is lack of cash or funding. You confide in Phil that you had a divorce a couple years ago that ruined your credit. You tell him that you are working to rebuild it so you can get bank loans, but they are not an option right now. You tell him that you have $40,000 that you have saved that you could use, but you haven't found any houses in that price range. Phil then says that he has $40,000 in a savings account earning 2% that he would like to put to work. Phil recommends that you both put up the money, and both have a say in all aspects of the business, and you both agree that you will both be 50/50 member/managers of the LLC. You go to a corporate attorney and pay her a few thousand dollars to draft an operating agreement for your new entity. You and Phil give the company the funds, and you find a great house for $60,000, and your Realtor pulls comps that show a retail price of $110,000 and a rental value of $800 a month. Phil goes and looks at the home. He has a contractor that he trusts whom he calls to come give an estimate of repairs. The contractor gives a repair esti-mate of $15,000 for carpet, paint and a few doors and windows. You both decide that there is profit to be made, so you both sign an offer and your Realtor submits it to the bank's broker. A few days later, the bank comes back with a counter offer. You talk to Phil on the phone and both of you decide to move forward with the deal. You purchase the home for $65,000.

After the repairs are completed, you do a lease/purchase on the home for $110,000 in sales price and a lease of $800 a month during the 1st year. After property taxes and insurance, you are netting $500 a month cash flow since you are using equity instead of debt. You don't have to pay the bank interest, thereby increasing your return. You also instantly increase your net worth by $15,000 once the repairs are completed. You both now have $55,000 equity, your original $40,000 investment and the $15,000 equity you have created, in the home and have a potential $3000 each in passive income. Once the home sells, you will make a profit of around $19,900 after paying Realtor fees and $3500 in closing costs for the buyer. You have made $5400 in rental income after replacing a water heater for $600 during the year. So you have an annualized return of around 31% on your money. Not bad!

Now let's turn it up a few notches. The true way to get very wealthy in real estate is to syndicate deals by selling shares or units in your company to passive investors. Here, you are truly creating money out of thin air with your business and real estate knowledge. I have used this method many times in the past, and it is my favorite way to invest. Here is an overview of how it works.

You notice that real estate prices in your area have fallen quite a bit and have heard the rental demand is going to increase because of the difficulty the average person is having in getting a mortgage. You decide to go to a seminar that is being held in your city on investing in income producing properties. At the seminar you learn about syndicating real estate deals and the freedom that knowing this process can create. You learn that the best investors to work with are accredited investors. You learn that accredited investors are investors that have an income of at least $200,000 a year or $300,000 jointly with their spouse; or they have a net worth of at least $1 million dollars. You learn that you must have a preexisting relationship with your accredited investor and that you cannot do a general solicitation. You learn about the SEC and its involvement in private placement investments.

During a break, you are networking with one of the other attendees Brenda. She tells you that she has done several syndications but keeps coming back to the seminars because she always picks up one good idea. She also tells you that if you are going to syndicate a deal, she has a great securities attorney that she would recommend. You thank her for her advice and write down the attorney's name and phone number.

When you leave the seminar, your head is spinning. You think of all the money that you can make for investors with the properties you have seen on the market. You get excited about the opportunity to start a company and sell shares of it for equity to fund your deals. You start thinking about the magnitude of selling stocks and how all it really takes to make money is a good idea and a great plan. Then it hits you. A family friend, who is an optometrist, Dr. Jones, has mentioned some real estate investments to you during barbecues you have attended. You have both discussed the market and strategies for making money. He even complained that he knew there were great deals to be had in this market; he simply didn't have the time to find them.

The next day you call Dr. Jones' office and leave a message for him. He emails you back and wants to have lunch the following week. In the meantime, you call the securities attorney that Brenda from the seminar recommended. The attorney calls you back and schedules a conference call for that Friday at 10 a.m. to talk about what you want to accomplish and how you see your deals being structured. At 10 a.m. you start the call.

First she asks you general questions like what you are up to and what you want to accomplish. You tell her that you have a couple of properties that you are looking to purchase and that you have a family friend who has shown an interest. You tell her that you want him to be a passive investor and for you to have all the management rights in the company. She asks you pointed questions about how you know him and how long you have known him. "Does he live in this state?" she continues. She also asks you questions about the properties you are considering and the stage of your interest or offers. Then you complete the call, and she starts working on the Operating Agreement and Subscription agreement.

After the call, you look for properties and find a small three bedroom two bath foreclosure that has been on the market for 187 days and has been under contract before, but the contract fell apart. Your Realtor once again has pulled comps for both for sales and rentals and comes back with some interesting details. The home could be rented for $975 a month and has a retail resale value of somewhere around $120,000. Since the home has been on the market for quite some time and has been under contract before, you feel that you have a pretty good chance of getting a low offer accepted. You decide to discuss the house with Dr. Jones.

During your lunch meeting, you have Dr. Jones sign an accredited investor form. You tell him about the property you have been looking at and go through the potential numbers of the deal. He tells you that he is interested and asks you how much money he needs to get in. You tell him you won't know for sure until you have the home under contract, but you think a minimum investment of $70,000 will be needed. He tells you that will be no problem and that he wants in!

You leave the meeting feeling great. You have a commitment from your first equity investor. Then you realize that you need to make an offer, but you still don't have any money. You come down from your high and head back to your office to transfer some of your personal money into the business account to pay for the earnest money. You call your Realtor and tell him to make an offer of $58,000. Your Realtor tells you that you are crazy and that the seller, a bank, is never going to accept an offer that low. The Bank is currently asking $89,000 for the house. You tell him to proceed with the offer and make it a cash offer with a two week close.

The next day the Realtor calls and tells you that the bank has accepted your offer! You are extremely excited and start thinking of all the things you are going to be able to do with your $15,000 or so profit from this deal. Then you remember you only have a promise for money. You don't actually have any money yet. You call Dr. Jones to tell him the good news. You now have a property for him to invest in, and the return looks great! Dr. Jones sounds less than thrilled. He tells you that while he still wants to invest with you, he got a call from his daughter in college last night. She was in a wreck and totaled her car. The good news is that she is okay. The bad news is that until he sees how much the entire event is going to cost him, he doesn't want to commit his currently available cash.

You tell him you understand and that you are glad his daughter is okay. You are sitting at your computer and are wondering what in the world you are going to do now. You thought you had it made a few hours ago. Now you have a house tied up with no way of closing, and your earnest money is on the line. You remember that Mac, a long-time friend of the family, has always been interested in investing, and you have spoken to him about his investments before. You remember him talking about private placements for companies, so you start to think he might be a good person to pitch. You give him a call, and he invites you to lunch at his club. He says he will be finished with his round at two, and he will meet you on the deck.

You print another Accredited Investor form as well as your subscription agreement and operating agreement. You put together the spreadsheet you get from me by emailing kyle@freemeforever.com with "Free Spreadsheet" in the title. The spreadsheet shows your purchase price, the monthly income and expenses and your exit strategy. You figure that if you hold the home for one year and can sell it for $109,000, then you will make a gross profit of around $28,960. You are going to pitch splitting the profit 50/50 with Mac, which will make his return around 21%. You look over the numbers and get pumped up for your meeting.

You sit down on the deck of the country club overlooking the 18th green. The white tablecloths are blowing in the breeze. It's Tuesday afternoon, and you are amazed at all the people who seem to be hanging out. The waiter pours your water as Mac walks up and shakes your hand. You tell him it's great to see him and thank him for letting you come to meet him so quickly. You jump right in and tell him your situation. You know that you should probably be more reserved about your position, but you just want to tell someone, and you feel like Mac will understand. He sits and listens to you patiently as you hurry through your story about the doctor, your earnest money and the closing date that is fast approaching. When you are through, Mac folds his arms and smiles, "I am proud of you," he says as if he doesn't understand the situation you have gotten yourself into.

You take that to mean he will help you, and you tell him that you have an Accredited Investor form for him to fill out and tell him that he will get 50% of your company for the $70,000 equity contribution and that you have enclosed a copy of the operating agreement and subscription agreement for his review. He says that he is excited, and he will look over it, but he wants 75% of the profit, not 50%. He says that he knows that you need the money and don't have much of a choice, and he says, "Honestly, this is a small return compared to the start ups I usually invest in, but I admire your courage and resourcefulness so I will give you this $70,000 and let you keep rolling it over for a few years to see what you can do."

Although you are a little depressed because half your profit just disappeared, you are excited that you finally got your money, or at least a firm commitment, and now you can close and honor your contract. You like the fact that you have the money to roll over and can now count on having this money if you can turn the house you have under contract. You start to see the value of turning the houses quickly instead of holding out for top dollar. You have also realized that you should always raise at least twice as much money as you need, because something will always come up and someone, no matter how good their intentions, will not be able to keep their commitment, and when they don't, it is your problem. You also start to see how this could be a way to create urgency. If you have more than enough money lined up for your deals, then when you announce the deals to your investors, you can say things like, "The first people to get the money wired into my account will be in this deal; the others will have to wait until the next one." You also can't help but think how you can tell Mac that you don't want his money anymore for 75% ownership. You have other investors who only require 50%. For now, you are happy to be moving forward with your close and can't wait to wake up in the morning and check the bank account for the wire.

As you can tell by reading this chapter, there are key things to know when you are raising private equity and debt. This chapter is an introduction to the concepts of raising money. For more information, please visit www.freemeforever.com.

CHAPTER 7

BANK MONEY

Most people think getting money from a bank is pretty straight forward and simple. They assume that if you have good credit, a steady job with some job time, and money in the bank, then you can get a loan. Otherwise, you will only be turned down. Although this common ideal is not entirely untrue, it over-simplifies the reality that banks are a valuable source of funding and can be used profitably.

In getting a loan from a bank, probably the toughest hurdle to clear will be bad credit. If you have established a repeated pattern of not paying your borrowed funds back, you will have great difficulty in convincing business bankers that things will be different in the future. There are a few steps that you should take no matter what your current situation to improve your chances of getting the loan approved.

First, I will clarify that getting a loan for real estate investment is not the same thing as getting a mortgage. As a matter of fact, I don't have a mortgage loan on any of my properties. From the very beginning, all my loans originated on the retail or commercial side of the bank, not the mortgage department. What's the difference? For starters, mortgages are bought and sold on the secondary market, and since the jumbo and subprime collapse in 2007 and 2008, secondary markets or investors are extra picky about who participates in the pool.

When you apply for a mortgage today, you have to provide a ton of paperwork, and you usually have to have the three things I mentioned: job, money and credit. You will probably need a good job with job time, documented income and a certain amount of money in savings to cover initial purchase expenses, and a high credit score. If you stay away from the mortgage lending department and deal directly with a business banker, or a retail lender such as a branch manager, then your paperwork and burden of proof can be considerably lighter.

Armed with this knowledge, why would you ever get a mortgage on a particular property? Well, as I mentioned, I haven't. I started by getting retail loans for my first property, quickly setting up companies for the following properties for liability, and also so I could work with a business banker. I wanted to be on the business side of the bank. However, there are advantages to having a mortgage. While I'm not sure the positives outweigh the negatives, in your circumstances, they might.

On the plus side, a mortgage typically has a 30 year term, amortized over a 30 year period. This keeps your payments lower. Retail loans and business or commercial loans are typically amortized over a much shorter period, usually 15 to 20 years, but I have had some as short as 10 and as long as 25. Normally, you will negotiate this point with your business banker.

Mortgages also usually have lower interest rates than retail, business, and commercial loans. Mortgage rates have remained in the 4% to 6% range since I have accumulated my properties. During that period, the interest rates on my business loans have ranged from 3.5% to 7.25% depending on the structure. Overall, mortgages are much less flexible in terms and approvals than other types of loans, but if the terms and loan approval requirements meet your needs, they may be the least expensive way to acquire property.

Something else to consider when you weigh your options between a mortgage and a different bank source is that most mortgages have higher closing costs than a retail or business loan. This results mainly for the extensive processing. For instance, mortgage brokers might charge you one percent of the loan amount as a loan origination fee; one of my business bankers only charges me .25%. Also, with a mortgage you will have to get an appraisal, maybe two, which costs anywhere from $250-$500 each. (Most of my business bankers, however, will use the tax value as the basis for the loan, and since I buy most of my properties at a deep discount to tax value, they let me slide without an appraisal.) Last, from my own experience, I have never seen a mortgage issued in a corporate name. This means that you must hold the property in your personal name, which I would avoid at all costs. The amount you save is pennies compared to your increased risk. In short, if you cannot make the numbers work on the property using a business loan or commercial loan, then the property is probably not a great deal, and you should keep looking. If it's simply a "must have," then you'll want to seek private funding, preferably equity.

So now that we have decided that mortgages are only the best option in a few circumstances, let's move on to business and commercial loans. For the sake of simplicity, I will call both of these loans business loans from now on. Banks use the terms interchangeably with some calling it their "commercial" loan department and others the "business banking" department. A few quick questions to a teller or a receptionist should get you pointed in the right direction.

To work with a business banker, first you need to have or establish a business. You'll choose your business structure according to the purpose of your business, and a corporate attorney can be a big help here, as well as a CPA. If you do not have a CPA or a solid attorney on your team, then you need to go ahead and start looking for them. Remember, cheap is not always less expensive, and when it comes to tax and legal advice, playing it cheap is absolutely the wrong way to go. But with that said, don't let the idea of starting a business scare you. It's really very simple. You just need a name that can be registered, and an attorney and CPA to help you with the correct structure and documents. Of course, you can set these up on your own, but I would never recommend that.

So what exactly is a company? Put simply, it is an entity that conducts business. To start with, it is a name, legal documents, and a tax id number. Then you add a bank account and order deposit slips and checks. Next, you either fund the account with a contribution from yourself or other investors, and you have a business. This is the stage you want to reach before approaching a business banker. All set up, at this point, you start to look like you mean business. No longer just talking about it, you are acting, creating it as a reality.

If you know what bank you plan to approach, it would be helpful to set up the business checking account at that bank first. If you don't know which bank you plan to target, then you might want to interview a few bankers before setting up a checking account, or be prepared to set up multiple checking accounts at the different banks used by the company. The latter is the strategy I use. I have multiple checking accounts for the same company at the various banks I am using at the time. If I stop using a bank for an extended period, I simply close out the checking account. I have had as many as 12 checking accounts for the same business open at the same time. Does it get confusing? It can. Is it worth it? Of course! You are keeping your banker happy and getting more money!

Once you have your company set up, you need to find a property and a banker, two tasks you should work on at the same time. Ideally, you will identify a banker and take a property under contract to your first serious meeting. I have found that this gets things moving along at a quicker pace, as well as it makes you look like a serious investor who gets things done. The only risk is that the bank may say no. If the banker does, you should have other banks lined up and also be working your private money contacts so that you can still put the deal together. With that being said, I have had appealing deals under contract when I was unable to find funding. Rarely, but it has happened. Over the past few years, I have probably put 25 of my 30+ houses under contract without knowing exactly where I was going to get the funds. Of all those deals, I have only had to forfeit earnest money twice. Both were $500 deposits. I lost them because I made cash offers to get the best possible price, but then could not find funding before the offer expired. I tell you this so you will know that losing earnest money is not the end of the world. If you don't lose some every now and then, you are probably not pursuing deals aggressively. If you do lose some earnest money, just move on. Don't let it shake your confidence. Just keep moving.

A common misconception of most people is seeing all banks as pretty much the same and thinking that if one tells you no, then the others will too. Especially in today's financial markets, nothing could be further from the truth. The bank that funds all your deals this week might cut you off next week. The bank that told you no only a few weeks ago might have money to lend tomorrow. You will need to establish a network of bankers at multiple banks and work them regularly to find out who is the best person to put the next deal together.

Most of you are probably familiar with the large, nationwide banks. While in the past, these have been great places to get money; however, if you are looking for business money for real estate today, these banks are not where you want to go. In fact, I have gotten 100% of my bank loans from regional and local banks. This means that you will have even more banks to sift through, as the majority of the regional and local ones will probably not offer the right fit for what you want to do.

With all these banks to choose from and all these banks to sift through, where do you start? I would recommend that you start with a friend or family member in the banking business, no matter what his role, or a person you know at your personal bank, even if he is a teller. If you don't know anyone, then you might go to local bank websites, find the names of the branch managers, and call them. You should continue to call different banks until you have at least three appointments set up or substantial phone conversations.

Often I will use the following phrase: "Can you refer me to the person who can help me with my business real estate loans and opening the operating accounts?" When I get in touch with that person, I ask, "What is your appetite for income producing real estate right now?" This allows him to take the stage and present to you. It will also give you an idea right away of whether or not the relationship is going to meet your needs. If he says that he is not giving new customers real estate loans right now, then you should evaluate your priorities. Do you have a home under contract that you are trying to close this month? If so, you should probably keep moving down your call list to other banks.

Even if the banker turns you down, always ask if you can call him back to schedule a time to meet, so you can tell him about what your company is doing and the opportunities you see in the market. Then you can keep in touch to see if and when his policies change. Remember, even when you aren't getting money, making the personal connection is important. If you don't yet have a property under contract, then you should see if you can stop by the next day to say hello and go over the business plan. The main objective is to build a solid network of bankers who know you.

If you do know someone in the business, take him to lunch. Get him excited about your business plan: the holes you see in the market, how you are going to create and generate passive cash flow that will pay, no matter where you are or what you're doing. Sell him the dream. Make him feel your excitement. His role in the bank doesn't even matter; if you get him excited, he will tell others and spread your excitement. Ask him to refer you to the business banker in his branch, or network of branches. Ask for a personal introduction. If his bank does not currently have an appetite for income producing real estate loans, then ask whom he knows that might. Most bankers know other bankers and also know what other banks are doing. I have found them to be quite helpful in referring me to other bankers at different companies, when they know someone else who might better meet my needs. They know that the favor will come back around. I always give the referring banker the first shot at my business from then on out, even if they didn't do the original loan.

Another thing about banks: once you get a certain amount of houses, some banks will not like it, and others will. The funny thing is that, on the one hand, some banks will like you more when you are starting out without much money or experience, and once you get 10, 20, or 30 houses, they will start getting uncomfortable loaning to you, even if your houses are producing cash and you are paying as agreed. They will simply refuse to loan you anything that exceeds a certain dollar amount. On the other hand, some banks will prefer to loan money to a more seasoned investor and refuse to loan to someone inexperienced. The thing to remember is that banks are as unique as private investors. What one likes, the other doesn't. When one is lending, another is not. All this changes monthly, weekly, even daily. Therefore, you have to establish your network of lenders and stay on top of them. Making those personal connections, you should be able to have every banker in your markets know who you are and what you are doing as a goal.

Once you have a few bankers in your circle, then what? Well, you need to be prepared to present pertinent information to your banker. In doing this, you want to remember a few key points. First, you need a personal financial statement. Your personal financial statement will give the banker a snapshot of your personal finances. It is your personal balance sheet. For a free personal financial statement that you can use, email me at kyle@freemeforever.com and ask for the PFS. I will get it emailed out to you instantly.

Your personal financial statement will list all your assets and liabilities, totaling your net worth. Your Net Worth is your value; in other words, your assets minus your liabilities. Your net worth will increase rapidly as you start to buy properties. When someone says they are a millionaire, that doesn't mean they have a million dollars in an account, but that they have a million dollars or more as net worth. Your banker will use this number in deciding how much money to loan you. Ironically, if you use the correct formulas and buy income-producing properties, then every time you borrow money to make a purchase, your net worth rises.

On the personal financial statement, you will list all of your bank accounts. They will be separated by institution, bank, and the account balance. These balances will be your total cash on hand. You will also list all stocks, bonds, and mutual funds you own. You will list any whole life insurance policies and their amounts. You will list your stocks in closely held companies (mainly, your companies.) You will list all of your vehicles, equipment, and machinery. You will also list all of your personal real estate. You will list the value and any debt that you have against your vehicles, equipment, machinery, as well as your personal real estate. Once you have this in place, the spreadsheet will subtract your liabilities from your assets and render your net worth. If it is low or even negative right now, do not feel discouraged. By assessing your current situation, you have taken the first step toward achieving your success. Once you have a benchmark, you can update your financial statement every thirty days, enabling you to watch your wealth grow. If you get off track, your financial statement will let you know.

The second part of your package should include the last two years of your federal and state tax returns. This will give the banker an overall sense of your income, including the source. This is your personal income statement. I get my accountant to email a copy of my tax returns in PDF format. Then I can send it over to as many bankers as I need, quickly and easily. If you do your own taxes, stop, unless you are a CPA. Find a CPA who can help you. If you don't know one, ask your attorney or a business banker for recommendations. Even if you can do your taxes without any trouble right now, once you add a few income producing properties, you will want professional guidance. It will more than pay for itself.

The third section is your property package. I use a Property Analysis Worksheet, which you can get from me free by emailing kyle@freeme-forever.com. Over the past three years, I developed this spreadsheet while I analyzed hundreds of properties. It is developed so that you can evaluate properties quickly and efficiently without forgetting any of the details. Analyzing properties is necessary to buying properties right which is the key to making money.

With the Property Analysis software, you can analyze any property, large or small, commercial or residential, in just a few minutes, with just a few simple key strokes. You enter the amount you will pay, or think you should pay, along with your repair costs, tax and maintenance expenses, and loan information, as well as your income and exit strategy projections. The spreadsheet creates a profit statement, as well as an income statement, so that you can see very clearly if the property has positive cash flow. Enabling you to quickly estimate your work, I have included a construction cost page where you can load in your cost for each unit of a repair. For example, if you know that your painter charges you $1.25 per square foot, and your carpet runs $3 per square foot, then you can set the spreadsheet to give you a repair cost instantly by typing in the square footage of the home. When you analyze a property, this offers you a quick and accurate estimate, without having to get individual quotes each time or, worse, having to crunch the numbers manually.

In case you do not yet have your unit cost figured out, I have included my guideline cost per unit in the spreadsheet, so you can use them as a rough estimate. I would recommend, however, getting your own local figures in place as soon as possible.

Your banker will be highly impressed with the thorough analysis and the reports this spreadsheet provides. I have seen bankers' mouths literally drop open when I handed him this spreadsheet. He can't believe that I analyzed a single family residence in such acute detail. It gives them something to show their underwriters and helps make their job easier, which makes it easier for you to get the loan. A well-prepared property package takes the focus off you personally and places it on the property, which can be very important when you are starting out. If you are not yet strong financially, but have a strong property, the bank might overlook your personal deficiencies, focusing instead on the opportunity you've presented. This is the importance of the property package: it makes you look professional. It shows you have an exit strategy, separating you from all those people who walk in and say, "I want to buy this house so I can rent it and make some money."

The Personal Financial Statement, Tax Returns, and Property Package are pretty much standard and mandatory with all banks and loans, but there is one optional piece that I like to include: a business plan or a biography. This lets the bank know who you are, and where you or your company is going. It will tell business bankers who is on your team, describe your goals, and how you intend to achieve them. Your biography tells them what you were doing before you walked into their office to ask for money and highlights the strengths of your past experience as they relate to your future. Big dreams with a realistic strategy let them know you can think big and back it up with a real world plan.

Once you have your Presentation Package together in a neat and easily presentable format, then you are ready to sit down with your banker. I prefer a PDF document for all four parts. Typically, I keep the four components separate in different PDF documents, and I do this for two reasons: first, it is easy for the banker to find what he needs. Second, it is not such a large document that you can't get it through the bank's spam filters. If you are presenting the package by email, I would recommend calling the banker after you send it, making sure he receives it, and then asking him for a conference call at a specific time to go over the documents. If you are presenting in his office, I would email the package right before the meeting, so he can review it if he likes, and I would show up with paper copies for everyone who plans to be present. For instance, if it is going to be you, your partner, and the banker, then you should take three paper copies. This way, everyone can follow along as you explain. I know this sounds like a picky detail, but nothing makes you feel quite as uncomfortable as sitting there smiling because you do not have a clue what your partner and the banker are talking about.

Once you have completed your presentation, ask the banker if this is something she would like to work on together. She might need to get approval from an underwriter, or she might be able to move forward right away. If she does hint to needing another person's approval, then ask when she might have a commitment. You want to be very confident in your language, always assuming that you will get the loan. Never ask, "Do you think I can get it?" Or, "Let me know if you can do it or not?" You should expect it to go through. Assume she can do it, that she will certainly want to do it, and just ask for a time frame. They are giving you the right to follow up on that day. For example, if she tells you that it takes five days for the underwriter to process the loan, then call her on day six to see if she needs "any additional information." You must stay on the banker's mind, but never seem overbearing or annoying. By asking if she needs additional information, you are not asking if the loan is going to go through but simply offering help.

One other thing to remember is that bankers are typically conservative people. They have an exceptionally formal job that requires them to adhere to strict codes. They work structured office hours and usually don't work outside of those hours. Treat your bankers with respect and mirror them in your meetings. Dress as your bankers dress when you go to meetings, especially in their office. It will make you fit in, look like one of them, and mainly, not stick out. If your banker gives you her mobile phone number, only call it after trying the office during normal business hours, unless you are given expressed permission to do otherwise. Also, avoid bragging about the fact that you can wear anything you want and go a month without shaving or setting an alarm clock. These are the types of conversations you can save for your deep-pocketed angel investors, who are probably eccentrics themselves. Keep your conversations with your banker as conservative as your dark suit.

CHAPTER 8

FINDING THE GEMS

Especially in today's market, most people think they can easily find good deals, and they are right, but you have to know what to look for; often times, what appears to be a great deal is only a bad one in disguise. Sometimes a deal looks great on the surface, but once you know how to look beneath, as I teach you, you will see the truth. The reality is that most deals, even if they look appealing at first, are not great. These are the ones the average investor buys. These are the deals that prove difficult to resell for profit in today's market sitting vacant with "for sale" signs out front. These are the deals that require a strong fight to obtain financing for purchase. With these secrets, you can find the gems.

The deals I am going to teach you how to buy are like one I found a few months ago. The bank was asking $120,000. It sat on the market for a while, but the price dropped to $110,000 and finally $89,000. Most people would have thought they had found a great deal, especially since the tax value on the home was $180,000. And people did think it was a great deal. It went under contract several times while I sat back and watched. It would go under contract and then, pop back up on the market. The deal would never close. Why not? I don't know, exactly. There could have been many reasons. My guess is that the banker didn't get the right price, so financing was a challenge.

I ended up purchasing this home for $57,807. That's right, I purchased the home for over $120,000 under tax value. And here is the best part: the home only needed carpet, paint, and appliances. No major renovation, just some minor cosmetic repairs that I took care of quickly and easily. Here is another key element to the deal. A smaller, older home sold for $99,000 in that neighborhood just a few days before I closed on my purchase. I just sold that home for $106,000. I made a little over $30,000 in less than 90 days.

Why do I bring up this purchase and sale, specifically, out of the many deals that I have done? In particular, this one illustrates how easily you can get off track if you don't know the exact steps to follow. Most people would think that if you could buy a house for $89,000 with a tax value of $180,000 (which it did sell for in the past), then it's a good deal. This is where they would make a mistake.

So how do you avoid making these types of mistakes? First, you keep deals coming across your desk. That is what we will discuss in this chapter. As long as you have plenty of deal flow, you will not get caught up in trying to make one deal fit your needs. You need many deals so that you are not emotionally attached to one. As the old saying goes, to the hammer, everything looks like a nail. But if you have multiple tools, or multiple deals, you can choose the right one for the job.

Notice: when I started telling you about this case study, I mentioned that it had gone under contract several times as I just sat back and watched. This is a key strategy. If I had thought this was my only deal or only chance of getting a deal, then I would have seen the bidders in a different light. I would have thought they were my competition, and that I should bid against them. In reality, though, I saw them as my helpers. If they overpaid for the houses, they would provide a good comp for me when I wanted to sell my houses. Also, I would be able to rent and sell my houses much cheaper than they could. Therefore, I would sell mine first and also get a tenant first. If they put the house under contract and did not close, they would wear the bank down a little more. The bankers would count that house as sold in their monthly projections. They would see it as gone on their books, and then it would reappear, a thorn in their side that I can pluck for an excellent price. You see, as long as you have plenty of deal flow, you see everyone as an ally in some capacity. You can think strategically. Think through your deals and let others help you get the best ones. Your deal flow is the key to your success. If you don't have it, you will buy the first marginal deal that comes through, always fighting an uphill battle.

Imagine if I had paid $89,000 instead of $58,000 for the house I just told you about. How would that have changed things? Well, if I rented the house for $975 a month, the going rate in the neighborhood, then I could have a cash flow of approximately $200 a month if I had paid $58,000 and financed $70,000 for purchase and repairs. If I had purchased it for $89,000 and added the repairs for a total of $101,000, I would have a slightly negative cash flow at $975 a month. That would give me two options: charge more for rent or lose money every month. Option one, raising the rent would mean setting rent higher than the market price, which would mean I have a longer lease up period, which in turn would lower my cash flow because I would have it sitting vacant for months while I paid out of pocket. Further, an overpriced rental unit might sit empty indefinitely. The second option would cost me monthly cash flow. I would have to spend my own money every month to make the payment. It's obvious why this option is no good; among other things, this limits the number of houses I can own. How many houses could you buy if you had to pay $50 a month out of your pocket every month to cover the difference between your income and expenses? No matter what the number, it is a fixed number. You can only do so many. Now, let's assume you are making $200 a month cash flow per house. How many houses can you own? There is no limit. You will take all you can get. Either way you look at it, I don't want to be in this situation. If you don't have enough deals coming across your desk, you will be tempted to try to make marginal deals work.

Also, as I mentioned earlier, I sold this house for $106,000. How good do you think the next person felt when they bought this house from me for over $70,000 below tax value? Pretty darn good. Do you think that helped me sell it? Of course it did.

The other thing I mentioned in the case study was that another home had just sold in the neighborhood for $99,000, which brings up another important point. If you are buying a home in a neighborhood for the same price as the others, you are paying retail for the house. It doesn't matter what houses sold for in the past, or what they rent for now; if you are paying the same thing other investors are paying, or worse, the same thing owner occupants are paying, you are not buying below market. You are buying at the market price. Now, there may not be anything wrong with that strategy, depending on where you are in the market cycle and how much positive cash flow you can create, but here is the main problem: everyone else has the same opportunity as you. I want to be the one who can drop the price the most and still make money, the one who can lower the rent the furthest and still have positive cash flow. That way, I stay in control. I can be the first to rent my property if I want and the first to sell.

What does all this have to do with finding gems? First, it will give you examples of what can look like a gem but be deceiving. Real gems are harder to find. Most real gems have to be created as I will explain in detail in the next chapter, "Negotiating and Navigating."

For now, let's focus on how we can get our deal flow coming to us. There are many sources for good deals, and in today's market, some work better than others. Some will work better tomorrow, and some that work today will not work so well tomorrow. Does all this sound familiar? Sounds like the banking discussion, doesn't it? Well, it should. Real estate is a dynamic game, changing every day. Never getting too tied down to one strategy, you have to keep your options open. When you find something that works, it can be tempting to just drop everything else. While I would definitely advise you to focus on what works today, I would also advise you to keep testing new ways of finding deals so that when things change, as they always do, you can stay ahead of the curve. Let me give a step-by-step account of how I have found every one of my deals over the past few years.

Realtors have been a great source for finding deals, and over the past few years, the one I have used the most. They provide a valuable service for you as a real estate investor, and if you become someone they can trust and profit by, they will do much of the work of finding good deals for you. They can also help you stop chasing deals and by turning things around, make the deals start chasing you. This is when things become really easy. Once you prove yourself as a closer – someone who buys properties and closes on time – once you prove that you mean business, Realtors will call you with everything they get their hands on. Giving you options, deals will come across your desk all the time with plenty to pick through. This is when the quick analysis of the spreadsheet you received from me by email starts to really pay off.

Before talking about how to get the best deals from Realtors, let me give you a quick overview of how a Realtor gets paid. Most of you may already know how this works, but for those of you who don't, this is valuable information. Realtors typically only get paid when a sale closes. They get nothing for showing you around and emailing you properties, unless you buy something through that particular broker. There is usually a commission split between the buyer's agent and the seller's agent. If you go directly to the listing agent, i.e. the seller's agent, then he will typically get a larger commission or both sides. No matter how little work the agents seem to have done, never cut an agent out of a transaction. If they brought your attention to the deal, then pay them by using them to complete the sale. You want as many brokers as possible to bring you deals every day. That is the goal. If you are seen as someone who cuts out brokers, then they won't send the deals to you, making it very hard for you to be a successful investor. In other words, when you cut a broker out of a transaction, then the broker is not getting paid, and you're cutting yourself out of future deals.

Sometimes another Realtor will get swept up into making a commission and advise you to cut out the agent that brought you the deal or a buyer's agent who has been showing you around in a particular market. They will tell you that, to get this deal done, you need to cut out the other guy. This doesn't happen often, but it does from time to time. Let me tell you what will happen if you fall into this ploy. Your buyer's agent getting cut out is going to be furious and will tell everyone she knows; the other broker, the one who was your buddy when you were inking the deal, is now going to cut you off also. Sure, they may bring you a pocket listing here or there (a listing not yet on the market), but they are not going to send you deals that don't involve them or, in other words, take the place of your buyer's agent because they now know that you will cut them out when the tables turn. Even though they were in on the shady deal, now they don't trust you.

Here are a few tips for dealing with Realtors so that you make sure you get the best deals and a first look at the deals. When you start investing, you are only going to get to look at the deals that the other investors in their database have passed on. You have to earn the right to move up the list to the top spot. You can do this quickly if you follow the simple suggestions that follow.

First, never try to get an agent to reduce or forego commission. Many investors make this mistake, and it is the worst thing that you could possibly do. Many investors have a short sighted approach to investing and only think of cutting cost versus expanding revenue. They see cutting out the agent's commission as a way of saving money. But what they don't realize is they just cut themselves out of the loop on the next wave of good deals. If you become "that" investor, the one who is always trying to find a way out of paying a commission, then you will be the last to see the good deals. Real estate agents are a tight group, and they are quick to share stories of the person who tried to go behind them and purchase a property, or who tried to cut the commission after a property was identified. *Do not be that investor!* Even if you don't feel like the agent deserves the commission, pay it; then tell her what you are looking for in your next deal. Nothing gets a broker more motivated than receiving a check from your closing. Afterward, get ready for the phone to start ringing.

Second, always be pleasant to work with and don't waste a broker's time. If you are hard to deal with or call the broker to do small, insignificant things, then sooner rather than later that broker will start dodging your calls and deleting your emails. Brokers have plenty of people in their databases who waste their time with no regrets. It is your job to stay out of these two categories. Remember: you need brokers on your team.

Being hard to deal with does not mean buying properties that are not good deals. Being hard to deal with can be as simple as forgetting to return a phone call – always call a broker every time he sends a property to you, especially if it is a property you already know you aren't going to buy. Go over every deal that the broker sends you with the broker personally. Send him your spreadsheet, in PDF format if you prefer, and show him why the property doesn't make sense for you. Even if he emails you the deals, I would still try to give a call after I email the analysis back. Try to keep in constant contact, and let him know that you value the opportunity to look at the properties he sends. If you start analyzing the properties without responding when you are not going to make an offer, the broker will soon stop sending them. You must remember that you are not going to buy the majority of properties he sends you, so you must give him something for his efforts on each one. This is highly important because it's so easy to forget. When a broker sends you a property to consider, he has sent you a gift. The return gift should be your valuable feedback and analysis of the deal. As you share your feedback, your broker will start to understand what you are looking for, and he will start to send you only the best properties. But this will take time. Don't let him give up on you before you find the property that will make you money! Stay in contact and let him know you value his time.

One of the most frequent ways buyers become a pain for brokers is trying to renegotiate after the contract is in place and not closing or performing on specific dates. If you get the home inspection back and there are major things that you did not budget into your projections, then definitely ask for them to be addressed or ask for a credit at closing, but don't try to rake the seller over the coals just because a few minor things pop up on the home inspection. Also, if you have a time table in the contract, get things done by those dates. The last thing a Realtor wants to do is spend the afternoon rescheduling all the components of the closing because your lender failed to get the appraisal ordered on time. I know it's easy for you to say, "This is not my fault," but in the eyes of the broker, anything that goes wrong on your end of the closing is your fault, no matter which one of your teammates dropped the ball.

Another way to make sure you show respect for your Realtor's time is to always ride by the properties before you ask for a showing. This may not work if you are out of town. Have her pull comps for you, both sales and rentals as discussed before. Analyze the property and then go look at it. Always look at the property before you make an offer; typically, I make that the last thing I do. If all the numbers make sense as far as sales and rental comps, then what the house looks like is not all that important. A rule of thumb that I have used with smaller single-family homes is that a house built within the past 10 years will need $10k worth of work, and $10k more for every decade after that. So if a home was built after 2000, it will need $10k in work; 1990's, $20k; and 1980's, $30k. Of course, this rule is very crude, but it will provide the framework you need to have an initial run at the numbers.

The major point I am trying to make is this: when you are first starting out, don't make your Realtor spend the day driving you around to see a bunch of houses, unless you really think you're going to make an offer. Only use her time when you have a house that works on paper. Once you have purchased houses from her, you can use more of her time. Now I have a Realtor go look at houses for me before I spend my time to go look at them, but I contributed considerably to his income before I asked for these types of favors. In general, just treat the agent as you would want to be treated if you were in his shoes.

How do you pick a Realtor? Well, for the sake of getting the best deals, I would advise you to deal with a listing broker when you find the property on your own. I would also suggest that you get on the buyers list of all the REO listing brokers in your markets. REO stands for Real Estate Owned, a bank term for foreclosed properties. There will probably be a few brokers that get most of the REO listings in your market. Get to know who these brokers are, and get on their buyers list. They will not have any time to baby you as an investor because of the volume of properties that they will be handling, but you will be a valuable asset to them and get the first phone calls if you buy properties from them directly, allowing them to get both sides of the commission and close quickly with cash offers. Don't expect these brokers to weed through their listings to give you the ones that make sense to you. Just hope you are near the top of their list, so they give you the first shot at all the new listings they get. You can weed some out at first glance and run others through your spreadsheet to make sure they have potential.

A buyer's broker can be a great source of properties as well. If you have a buyer's broker on your team, she can find all the deals that come on the market meeting your parameters. The buyer's broker is the one whom you can slowly teach how you analyze deals, and she will be able to start to pick out what you are looking for, without wasting your time with deals that don't fit. I like to have one good buyer's broker bringing me deals in each market, and then I keep my name on the REO agents' list. Let me give you some words of caution here: never, and I mean *never*, go to the listing agent if your buyer's broker has sent you the listing. Always have her contact the listing broker for you. If you cut your buyer's broker out one time, you will never get another deal from her again. If it can even be perceived that she brought you the deal, then I would use her. Nothing will end this valuable relationship quicker than you cutting her out of a deal by going directly to the seller or listing agent.

There are two types of buyer's brokers I like to work with. First, the older, established brokers who have been in the market and business forever. They know all the players and other brokers, and they bring creditability to you because you are their client. They play golf or tennis with all the other top brokers and can get the deal done. Second are the young and hungry brokers, aggressive because they're just getting started. These brokers need to get something closed quickly. They will chase down every lead they can get their hands on to find the property you want. You will get emails and texts at 5:00 in the morning and 11:30 at night with properties for you to analyze. Both of these broker types are great assets.

I have had success with young and hungry brokers. They are the most motivated to find good deals, and with the right feedback, they can be developed into great assets for your team. However, there are disadvantages to both broker types. The older, established broker will throw you a few deals, and if you don't jump on at least one, then she will think you are wasting her time and move on. Also, you will have to prove that you are a serious buyer to this broker, which may be hard if you are starting out. The younger broker can be so aggressive and energetic that he can step on toes and upset others in his fast paced fury to get you a deal. He may also be out of the loop of the old timers.

I have my buyer's agent set up and run several database searches for me so that we can extract properties from the Multiple Listing Service. I will go over these so that you can have your brokers do the same. This could be the most valuable information in the book. Most, if not all, broker software services allow the agent to set up these searches for you, so that you get an automatic email whenever a new listing meets your criteria. Here are some searches I would suggest. First, I would have them set up my favorite search, the tax value spread search. This is a search that lets you put in a tax value range and a list price range. You can then search for properties that are significantly less than tax value. But before I go any further, let me emphasize this. You cannot use tax values as an accurate guide for the value of properties. You must use recent sales comps. Not homes on the market. Not pending homes. Not homes that sold a year ago. Sold and closed homes that sold in the last six months are your true comps and will give you a true value. The reason I recommend the tax value search is because it is the most productive search I am using right now. It allows you to slice through a large amount of data in a short period of time and look for outliers that could be your next investments.

I like to run the following parameters in my markets. You will have to vary yours to meet what is working in your market. I usually run a tax value of $100k or higher and a listing price of $80k or lower. I then drop the price on both values down by $10k until you get to $50k. I don't buy many properties if the tax value is less than $60k. I am sure there is someone out there making good money on those homes, but it's not me. I make my money on homes that I can purchase between $50k and $100k, 95% of the time.

Next, I would have my Realtor set up a days-on-the market search, known as DOM. Depending on how slowly your market changes, you could have him do 180 days or more, or 360 days or more. What you are looking for is a manageable list that you can analyze and make offers on. I do not hesitate to make 50% and 60% of asking price offers on these properties. They have been on the market for so long; most people have long forgotten about them. They will be pleased to have the activity, even if they don't like your price.

Another search you can have your Realtor run is a "keyword" search. In some databases, there is a category for the following key words: Foreclosures, Short Sales, Pre-Foreclosures, Bank Sales, Corporate Owned, and also some of the larger banks by name. If your markets are anything like mine, you will probably want to add more parameters than just those key words. If you run a search just for foreclosures, you will probably end up with a list that is too large to work effectively.

In addition to Realtors, many other ways can lead you to the great deals. However, I must admit, while I have tried some of these over the past few years, they have not produced any substantial results. As of today, I have purchased every home I have through a Realtor, just as I have described above. That does not mean I will not keep trying other avenues, but I would advise you to start with Realtor-listed, bank REO properties. This is the most clear-cut and time efficient way that I know for finding great deals in today's market.

CHAPTER 9

NEGOTIATING AND NAVIGATING

This chapter is dedicated to helping you learn how to negotiate the successful purchase of a property and to help you navigate the closing process. Profitable deals are made, not found. If you think that it is easy to find good deals, then you are not really looking at good deals. Good, solid, profitable deals are hard to find in any market, because no matter what the market is doing, you need to purchase properties below the current market value. If the market is in a Recovery or Expansion, you do not have to get as deep of a discount, but I would still advise that you purchase for less than the market value to give you a layer of protection. If you can sell your properties, if needed, for less than the current market value, you can liquidate any property you need to sell quickly. This can give you a good deal of comfort knowing that you can turn your properties to cash at any time.

Negotiating the purchase price is how I create the best deals. I very rarely pay anywhere close to the list price of a property. Most of the time, I purchase properties for somewhere between 55% and 85% of the list price. Recently, I have been purchasing properties closer to the 55% than the 85%. Again, I want to stress here that you should not buy a property because you can get it for 55% of the list price, or because it is 40% of tax value or any other reason other than that there are proven recent comps in the immediate area that justify a good rental cash flow and resell value. These are the only two reasons to buy a property – cash flow and proven resell value in today's market.

So how do you buy a property at 55% off list price? The easiest way is to let the property age for a while, 60 or 90 days before you make an offer. This means that the property is on the market for 60 to 90 days before you make an offer. Many real estate investors try to be the first to hear about a property once it goes on the market. They are very concerned about being the first to know, the first to get the email from the Realtor and so on. I have been able to get a good deal on a new listing every now and then because a bank will underprice a home, but very rarely. I concentrate more on aged inventory rather than new inventory. I like homes that have been on the market for a long time, not the ones that just hit the market this morning. How much do you think a bank or another seller is going to drop the price if the home has just been put on the market? Not much. If you rush in and put in a low offer on a property that just hit the market, chances are pretty good you are not going to get the offer accepted. What you might end up doing is setting the seller up to take another less "ridiculous" offer.

I have seen this happen all too often. When I was starting out, I too thought I had to be the first to jump on a property as soon as it hit the market. I would see it, do my analysis and then call the Realtor to make an offer. I would make my low offer, listen to the Realtor remind me that she just put the sign in the yard 5 minutes ago and sit back and wait for a response. Most of the time, I did not get one. Not even a counter offer. Then I would come up a few hundred and go at it again. After a few weeks of this, the Realtor would stop returning my calls, and I would see the house go pending with another buyer. I would have helped him get a better deal than he might by continuously low balling the seller, but he still did not get what I would consider a good deal.

How could I have done this differently? How could I be more effective? Well, this is a question I have learned I need to ask myself every day. So I did, and this is what I found, and it has worked beautifully for me. If you are going to make an offer on a home as soon as it hits the market, it should be because you know the property is worth the listing price, or that you are willing to pay 90% of the asking price, or that you have information which can logically influence the seller's decision to sell at your price. An example? On one occasion I purchased a house for $58,500. The tax value on the home was $100,000. It was a 4 bedroom 2 bath. It rented for $800 a month. A few weeks later the house beside it came up for sale for $89,900. I called the listing agent and told him I had just purchased the house next door for cash. I showed him the comp. I showed him pictures of the inside of the house I had purchased which was in better shape than the house he had on the market. I showed him a picture of the back door of his house, kicked open where vandals had entered to steal copper out of the HVAC unit in the attic.

I then made the argument that the house was worth no more than the house I purchased next door. They were both built in the same year, 4 bedrooms, 2 baths and the house I was negotiating on currently was in worse condition and getting worse by the day as vandals kept stripping it. Because of the situation, the bank agreed to sell me the house for $58,500. I closed with cash within 7 days. The home was only on the market a few days. I had negotiated a sales price of 65% of the list price. How was I able to do this? Fear and urgency in the bank!

I could make the point that the bank could not get the house to appraise for anywhere near the asking price because I had a 60 day old comp sitting right beside the house at $58,500. Also, and probably the most convincing aspect, was that the house was being vandalized, so every day the house sat vacant, there was less of a house to sell. I gave the bank an easy solution to the problem. Sell the house to me, the vandals would be my problem, and I would pay cash so that the appraisal was not an issue. Also, the end of the month was fast approaching which meant the bank could close out the month with this property off the books!

This example is the exception. I do not negotiate most of the properties I purchase this way, but there are a few, so you should keep it as a tool in your tool box.

My favorite way to negotiate properties is dealing with aged inventory. This is a much less stressful way of buying properties. Let's think about this for a moment. It is kind of like the laid-back Warren Buffet type of investing versus the stressed-out day trader. If you need your properties to age before you buy them, then there is no hurry to do anything. Properties come on the market, and you go look at them when you get around to it. You don't worry about hopping in the car and being the first investor on the scene. You don't sit up until 2 a.m. hitting refresh on your email to see if any of your Realtors have sent you the new listings for the day. You just casually go about your life, buying properties on your terms whenever it pleases you.

I don't worry about looking at the property listings every day because I know that it is not where I find my best deals. My favorite property report? The "back on the market" report. Specifically, houses that have been under contract with other buyers and not closed. I would estimate that 75% of the homes I have purchased over the past two years were under contract with someone else before I purchased them. Doesn't that bring you relief? You don't have to be the first person to see a home and make an offer. As a matter of fact, you can let someone else see the house first and make an offer. All the other people looking at houses are your allies, not your competitors. They are helping set you up for success. Now, I admit, you will lose some houses you want because an owner occupant or another investor pays too much for the house, and they do close. But you will be surprised when you start looking at the pending houses by how many of them do not close. You will be even more surprised by how little the sellers will take to get rid of these problem properties that will seemingly never go away.

I can't tell you how many times I have put in an offer on a property that has not been accepted, only to have the property fall out of contract later on, and I end up purchasing it for less than my original offer. By the way, I always go back at a less purchase price on the second go-around. If there are multiple offers, I will go with my highest and best, but if I am the only one bidding on the property, which is most likely the case since so few people actually pay attention to the pending properties, I go in and try to get it for even less money now that I know everybody anticipated it being sold. This is the perfect way to purchase properties!

Just think about it! You get to leisurely look at properties on your own terms; knowing that if your offer doesn't get accepted now, you can possibly get another chance. You don't worry if other people are making offers on the same property. You just do your analysis, put your number on the offer, and submit to the seller. You don't get up every morning and rush to the computer to check to see which properties were listed that day, hoping to beat all the other investors doing the same thing. You simply check to see if your target properties that have gone pending are closed once a week or so and when you see one pop back out on the market, you make an offer. More than likely, you are the only person that noticed this property at all.

Here are a few suggestions when dealing with properties that have been under contract. One, the longer the property was under contract, the lower your offer can be. If the property was only off the market for 7 days, then you are probably not going to be able to steal it for 30% of asking price, but if the property has been under contract for 45 days or more and not closed, then I think you have a good chance of getting it for 60% or so of the asking price with a solid contract and a 14 day cash close. This brings me to another point. The best way to make the most profit off these deals is to make solid offers with quick cash closings. If you try to go at the seller with a 30 day close contingent on financing, a home inspection and on and on, then don't be surprised if you lose out to another investor who offers less money but shorter terms. Typically, a seller in this position is not looking for the most money, but the surer terms. If he can get his money now, he will take $5k or $10k less rather than having the risk for 30 or 45 days.

In addition to pending properties that do not close, you can also get great deals from aged inventory that has not been under contract before. If it has just been priced too high or has some other glaring problem that you can fix, make them a low offer as long as you can fix the problem. These sellers are usually easy to work with on terms also. If you have a seller who has been trying to sell the property for 180+ days with no offers, a weak offer with conditions and an extended close will be a welcome change. An offer with conditions and a 60 day close will at least give him hope in getting the property closed. These can be great targets on your first properties when you need an out if you can't get your financing lined up, or if you need more time to get your investors excited about a specific property.

In general, when negotiating, put yourself in the other person's shoes. Try to think of what he is wanting. Then try to give it to him. Remember, it must be a win/win situation for the deal to go through. If you are only trying to "win" for yourself, you will be facing an uphill battle. Yes, the seller wants the highest price for the property, and you, the buyer, want to buy it for the lowest price possible, but there are many other components to the deal than just price. Analyze the deal, find out what your price needs to be, then figure out what you can give the seller to get your price. It's a fun game and a very profitable one too! While everyone else is out looking for good deals and thinking strictly of themselves, you can create your own deals and negotiate them with very little competition.

So now that you have the property under contract, what do you do next? If you have a Realtor helping you, then he can tell you the appropriate steps for closing in the state or country you are purchasing the property. I will give you a general guideline over the next few paragraphs. However, remember that these vary from state to state.

You will need your lending source, which we have already discussed in detail. You will need a closing attorney in most states to represent you at the closing of the property. You will need Title Insurance to protect you against title defects in the property. You will need property insurance for the property with any lenders or lien holders listed on the insurance for their protection. You will need a termite inspector to inspect the home for damage. You will need a property inspector to look over the property and check all the systems. You may need a contractor to give you bids on your repair costs. You will probably want to get an appraisal of the property, although as I have discussed, you might not have to get an appraisal if you are using private funds or if the tax value is high enough and your business banker is comfortable with using that value. If your property is in a neighborhood with an HOA, you should contact the President to make sure there are no outstanding or upcoming assessments and to get a copy of the budget to make sure you are not buying into a broke HOA.

A good Realtor and attorney can help you through most of these steps and provide good references. Going through the motions of closing the property is the easy part. In my opinion, you have reached the summit of the mountain with an accepted contract, now it is all downhill from here. You still have to watch your step and make sure you are on the right track, but if you approached your climb with the right knowledge and partners as I have described in this book, it is a sunny descent from here.

CHAPTER 10

ANALYZING THE PROPERTIES

One thing is for sure, just because you find a foreclosure that is selling for half of what it did three years ago doesn't mean that it's a good deal. As a matter of fact, determining if a property is a good deal and acquiring it for a good deal are the most important aspects of investing. Included in this exercise is estimating your repair cost, and maybe even harder, estimating what you are going to need to do to the house to get it in selling shape. As I have eluded to in other parts of this book, it is all too easy to take a home that is a marginal deal and convince yourself that it's a great deal and then spend too much money on the rehab because you did not anticipate repairs, or more commonly, you decide to make it your pet project and put in granite counter tops and a pool in a working class neighborhood.

The most common mistake I see among beginners is they put too much money in the wrong places when remodeling a home. I blame it all on the "flip this" T.V. shows and also on our human nature which makes us want to do things that are creative and fun. I don't discourage using your creativity. As a matter of fact, it is essential if you are going to flourish in this business, which I intend for you to do. You just need to focus your creativity on producing a quality finished home that matches the neighborhood while staying within your budget. Remember, it is very easy to keep throwing money at something and make it nice. It does not take a real estate investor to do that. It does take more knowledge, principles that you are learning in this book, to find a home that can be negotiated to a fair price, understand the standards of the neighborhood and market, remodel the home to meet those standards while staying in your budget and selling or renting the home quickly so that you maximize your return. This is true creativity. You have to be much more creative to make $20k to $30k on a house in 90 days during a recession than to making a house look "great" by spending too much money on it and ending up owing or investing more than you can get in the market for the property.

Let's go through all the things you have to keep in mind and analyze when purchasing a home to rent and resell in today's market. Remember, I have software that will help you through all of this quickly and easily and maybe even more importantly, keep you from forgetting something and making a costly mistake. However, we are going to act as if you don't have the software for the rest of this chapter so we can go through all the specifics.

The first thing that we need to analyze is the local market that we are considering investing in. We do that by figuring out what market phase the market is currently experiencing. If you need to refresh your memory, go back and reread Chapter 6 "Analyzing the Market." Now that we have our overall strategy in mind, we need to find a house that we can start negotiating on, see Chapter 8 "Finding the Gems." Then once we find a few that look promising on the surface, we must dig a little deeper to see what's really there. Here is my rule of thumb. If my gut tells me it's a good deal, I run through all the numbers to make sure my gut is right. If my gut tells me that it is not a good deal, I don't bother with the numbers because I don't want to try to convince myself that I should buy a deal just because I can make the numbers work. If you try hard and long enough, you can manipulate the numbers and make any deal seem like a good deal. Don't do this. Stay objective. Always remember that there is another deal around the corner.

So what do we analyze? We first must gather the information of our subject property.

General

What is the address including zip code? MLS #? Subdivision name? How many bedrooms and baths? What is the square footage? What repairs need to be made? Flooring? What types? How many square feet? Roofing? Paint? Interior? Exterior? Windows and Doors? Landscaping? Plumbing? Heating and Air Conditioning? What year were the systems made/installed? Appliances? Drainage issues? What are the repairs going to cost (approx.)? What is our strike price (anticipated contract price)? What are the property taxes? What are the insurance costs? Does it need flood insurance? Is there an HOA? What are the dues and how often are they paid? Are there any pending assessments? What other monthly, quarterly and yearly expenses will I have to pay? Water? Trash? Lawn maintenance? Snow removal?

Funding

What is financing like right now? Am I using private money or bank money? If I am using private money, am I going to use equity or debt? What terms do I think I can negotiate? If I am going to use bank money, what are the terms for the loan I am going to need? What is the interest rate? What is the length of the note? The amortization? Will I just have the primary loan or will I have a credit line or equity line on this property? Am I getting a loan for construction cost or self funding those? How will the draws be set up? Will the bank require an appraisal? Can we just use tax value? What will my closing costs be for the loan structure being used?

Operating

What will my annual income be on the property?

What will my estimated Vacancy & Credit Allowance look like? 5%, 10%, 20%

What will my monthly, annual recurring expenses look like? (Use the list below for a reference.)

Accounting
Advertising
Marketing
Insurance

Janitorial Service

Lawn/Snow

Legal

Licenses

Miscellaneous

Property Management

Repairs and Maintenance

Resident Superintendent

Supplies

Taxes

Trash Removal

Utilities

What will my Net Operating Income be?

What will my debt service be? First Loan? Second Loan? Construction Loan?

What do I have left (cash flow!)? Hint: This should be a positive number!

Refinance

When will I have to refinance the property? What will be the estimated value at that time? What amount will I need to refinance the property? What will be the loan to value of the refinance? Will I get all my cash invested out of the property? Will I be able to take any equity out of the property without jeopardizing cash flow? What will be my new interest rate? What will be my adjusted cash flow?

Sales

When do I anticipate selling the property? What will be the sales price? How much commission will I pay? What will be my closing cost associated with the sale of the property? What, if any, closing cost will I pay for the buyer? What other concessions will I make to the buyer? What will be my loan/equity? payoff/payback?

Buyer's Funding Options

What type of loan will the buyer be able to get? How much will he have to put down? What will his interest rate be? What will his monthly payment be? Taking that into consideration and today's under-writing standards, what will his household income need to be?

Once you have the answers to most of these questions, you will have all the information you need to paint a realistic picture of your invest-ment. Then you can decide if it is a good use of your money or if you should move on to the next deal. Of course, you do not have to have the answer to every question to be able to evaluate a property. But if you can get all the information, especially at first when you are just learning the process, you will eliminate unnecessary risks.

Let's take a minute to run through the groups of questions I have proposed and discuss them. First, the general questions: the address, subdivision, bedrooms and baths and square footage are necessary so that you can have your Realtor pull comps for you. These are the things he will need to know to be able to give you accurate comparable sales. As we have discussed earlier, you need to have Realtors pull sold and rented comps, pending comps, current sale and rental comps and recently withdrawn listings. Hopefully, you can get at least three in each category. This will help you to get the full picture of what is going on. Once you have the comps, you must determine what condition the properties were or are in. The currents are easy because you can go look at them, if needed, although I would go through the analysis first to make sure you have an attractive deal before spending your time. For the sold and rented comps, you will have to rely on MLS comments to understand the condition. Keep in mind the comments are being used for marketing purposes and probably exaggerate the condition. Also, pay attention to how many are investor sales versus owner occupant sales. If there are a lot of investor sales, pull the comp where they pur-chased the house or search the tax records if necessary. Are you getting a better deal than they did? You should be!

Once you have a good understanding of the condition and prices of comparable rentals and sales, then you will need to get a better under-standing of what it will cost to bring your potential property up to sale-able or rentable condition. One thing to keep in mind is that your home will attract tenants and buyers based on its condition. If you have a dirty house or overgrown lawn, it will attract less desirable buyers and ten-ants. This doesn't mean that it must have the best finishes, but it does mean that the paint should look new, the carpet and floors should look new or at least clean, and the yard should be in top shape. Also, blinds can really add or detract from a house. I usually buy new cheap mini blinds and place them throughout the house. The cost is minimal, and it makes the home look much better from the street. Of course, no blinds are better than dirty or broken blinds. Make sure that you have all the blinds set the same. You don't want some open, some closed, some up and some down. Little things like this can make a huge difference with the first impression.

By giving your house new carpet, paint, appliances and blinds, you can sell your home faster than most owner occupant sellers whose house will have clutter filling it and worn finishes and appliances.

I typically do my repair estimate by square footage. I figure out what the going rate in the area is for painting, carpeting, roofing, etc. and then I use those per unit figures to give a quick estimate. Let me explain. When you call a roofer, carpet layer, painter, etc., to give you an estimate, they are going to come out to the house and measure the surface area they are going to have to replace. You will need to take this step for the first few deals that you do to get a good feel for the pricing. Once you have those numbers, I then divide them by the square footage of the house. Then I have a price per square foot based on the overall house square footage, not the surface area square footage. Then I can do a quick rough estimate without having to measure out the house.

For example, if I get a quote for the roof, flooring and painting on a 1300 square foot house and the estimates come in as follows:

Roof	$5500
Carpet and Vinyl Replacement (Entire House)	$2600
Painting Interior	$2000
Painting Exterior (Wood Siding)	$2500

Then I can divide the overall figures by the square footage of the house and figure out that the roofing will cost me $4.20 a square foot based on the homes square footage ($5500/1300sq ft). I will do this for all the figures to get my price per square foot. Then if I look at a similarly structured 1500 square foot home in the same city that needs a new roof I can approximate the cost at $6300 or $4.20 X 1500. Again, the software I have available will do these calculations for you and store them for you to make it very easy to analyze many deals in minimal time.

Once you have your estimated repair costs, then you can work your way back to the price you are willing to pay. Let's say that your comps tell you that this home will rent for $1100 a month and that a reasonable resell value with the repairs listed above is $134,000. You decide that you are going to try to resell this one with renting it out as your back-up plan in case it doesn't sell as quickly as you hope. You think you can negotiate a purchase price of $80,000 because the home shows very badly right now because of the chipped exterior paint, overgrown yard and badly soiled carpet with extreme pet odor. You have the repairs above to complete plus other odds and ends including appliances, so you anticipate having $25,000 in repairs. Will this deal work? Let's find out. Subtract the total cost of the property ($80,000 purchase price plus the $25,000 in repairs) from the net sales price ($134,900 minus commission, closing cost and expenses paid for the buyer i.e. closing cost). Let's go through the calculation.

Sales Price	$134,000
Commission 6%	$8094
Closing Cost	$1575
Buyers CC Paid	$2500
Net Sales Price	$121,831
Purchase Price	$80,000 (Strike Price)
Repair Cost	$25,000
Total Cost	$105,000
Net Sales Price	$121,831
Total Cost	$105,000
Profit	$16,831

If we purchased the home for $80,000, spent $25,000 on repairs, and estimated a selling price of $134,000 with Realtor commission at 6% of the selling price, we understand that in this market we are also going to have to pay some buyer closing costs to get the sale as well as the routine closing costs which results with a profit of $16,831. Is that enough? Well, it depends. If we are paying cash for the home and using our own money, (a scenario I find highly unlikely if you are following my advice), then it might be a good deal. If we sold it within the year, it would be a 16% return on our money, not bad. I think my first question at this point would be, "How aggressive or conservative is our estimated Sales Price. If it is $10 to $20k below other homes in the neighborhood, then I would probably continue to analyze with these numbers as guides. If the Sales Price was equal to or greater than other homes in the area, then I would probably want to lower my strike price before analyzing further. I am probably going to get low offers if I am not the lowest in the neighborhood. Let's assume that the former description is accurate. This is the perfect place to transition over to the funding questions before we can decide if we have a deal because we have to know where we are going to get our money and what we are going to have to pay for it.

We might have a deal identified, but we have to get our funding in order. How do we want to fund this deal? Because we have unlimited options and opportunities at this point, let's start to narrow them down. Let's assume we don't have any of our own money to invest and that we have had a job change recently that gave us a credit bump because we were 30 days late on a car payment. Now we are back to work, but at a less than desirable job, and you are ready to blaze the trail on your own. In this case private debt or equity would be the ideal way to go.

Let's assume that you have been going to your local Real Estate Investors Association meetings, and you met a guy about a year ago there who said he had equity to invest if you ever ran across a good deal and needed help. You chat with him when you go to the meetings, hoping to take him up on his offer one day. This is the day! You give him a call and have him fill out an accredited investor form. He fills it out and signs it, meeting the qualifications with no problem. You then begin to explain the deal that you have without telling him the address etc. unless you have the home locked up under contract, which at this point because it's our first deal, we don't. He looks at the numbers and explains to you that if you split the profit 50/50% as you are suggesting, his return is only 8% or so on his equity. (Profit of $16,831 divided by 2, you and him, then divided by $105,000 which is his equity investment.) He says he is looking for at least a 10% return. You get off the phone a little disappointed, but you realize that to get your money man a 10% return, you only have to get the house for $75,000 instead of $80,000. This ups your profit by $5000 and gives him a 10% return. You now have your strike price of $75,000.

You pick up the phone to call your Realtor and put in an offer for $67,500 so you have some negotiating room. You are happy because you know you can probably get the money if you can get the deal under contract. You also like the fact that with equity, you don't have a payment, so you do not have any interest costs while you are waiting to sell the property.

Now let's look at it from a different point of view. Let's say that you have a banker that you met at a real estate investment seminar with whom you have built a relationship. He tells you he can borrow 80% of the purchase price and the repair cost. You have some money sitting in a money market account earning 3% so you decide to use that as your down payment. So you put $21,000 down and use the bank's money to fund the rest. You get a 7% interest rate on a 3 year fixed rate with a 25 year amortization. Your payment is $594 and taxes and insurance will run you $1200 and $600 annually. If you pay $80,000 for the home, use our original numbers and sell the house in 6 months, you will have made $12,367. (Our original profit of $16,831 minus 6 months interest $3564, minus 6 months of property taxes $600, minus 6 months of insurance $300.) Now if you divide your profit of $12,367 by your original investment of $21,000 you get a leveraged return of 58% on your money-market money. Is this a good return?

The most important thing to always remember is no matter how much profit you think you can make, your property must be able to cover its debt service, taxes and insurance from rental income. If not, you are speculating, not investing.

CHAPTER 11

ASSET MANAGEMENT

You just purchased your first house! Congratulations! Now what? Well, you should already have the plan that you developed when you analyzed the house. If that plan calls for you to try to resell the house quickly, then you will need to follow the instructions in Chapter 12. If you are going to try to rent the home to hold it for a certain period of time to ride the market or to lessen your tax burden, then you are going to need to decide on a management strategy. My advice is to seek the help of a professional management company. They can help you as soon as you close on the property. Most can even handle the remodel and upgrade that need to be completed to get the home ready for renters.

The process of interviewing and hiring a property management company can be a little complex and time consuming, but it is a key process in making sure your investment is going to perform as it should. You can manage the properties yourself. Most people don't take my advice and start out trying to manage the properties themselves. I was the same way. At first, for some reason, you think that you are saving money by not getting a property management company. Let me assure you, you are not. You will spend much more money in time and stress than the property management company will charge you. As a matter of fact, I would be willing to bet that once you try to manage your own properties and compare the headache with the cost of the property management company, you will think it is a deal. I do. There is no way I would manage a property for what my property management companies charge.

How much should you be paying for a good property management company? Well, it depends on what the company is doing for you and how many units you have it managing. For full service management, which is what I use and recommend, you will pay between 3% and 10% for long-term monthly rentals. Short-term rentals such as vacation rentals will be a higher percentage. I have as many as 20 single-family rentals with one company and I pay 8% currently. Usually, if you have multiple units, then the company will cut the rate from 10% to 8% for single-family. You will probably need four or more to get the discount. However, I would ask for it with only two. If you have multi-family units, you should expect to pay between 3% and 8% depending on how many units your building or complex contains. If you have less than 10 units, then you are going to pay 8%, if you get over 10, you might get a slight discount, and you will pay 3% or 4% if you have a large apartment complex with 100 units or more.

Here is some insider information. Do not try to talk the management company down to paying less than the market rate for your property in your area. If you do this, you are shooting yourself in the foot. If you are a management company and you have several different rental properties in the area and one pays you 8% and the other pays you 6%, which are you going to rent first? Of course, the one that pays you more. So you see, you are actually hurting yourself when you talk a property manager (or Realtor for that matter) into accepting a lower commission for your properties. Pay them well and expect the best service. Pay them the market rate, find the best managers in the market, and see what owning a well-run machine is like. You go to the mailbox and get checks! It's a wonderful business.

If you choose to manage the property yourself, expect pure hell. You will find that your tenants' favorite time to call with "emergency issues" will be holidays. The runner-up awards go to when you are heading out of town with your family, weekends and late nights. Nothing is quite like getting an "emergency" call from a drunken tenant who is locked out of his house.

Another huge benefit of having a professional property manager is one more layer of protection against you as the owner. You have a professional who should run your property accordingly. Your tenants probably do not know who you are. You have a company that owns the property, and a property management company who manages it. This is the mark of a true professional investor.

How do you find the best property managers? The best way is to talk to landlords in your investment market and ask them whom they have used. Here is the secret to making these references work for you: They must be the same property type. If you need a property manager for single-family properties, then the best apartment manager in town will not be a good fit. In addition to property type, you must also find a property manager who manages the same grade of property that you have. You do not want an A manager managing your C property. If you do, a couple of things will happen. First, he will spend too much of your money fixing up the property to meet the standards of the A clientele he is used to working with. Second, he is going to over screen your tenants, and you are going to end up with vacant units. Each property grade has its own unique finish and qualification standards. If you are not in line with both of these in your market, then you are going to have problems in the form of high vacancies or high expenses, two things you want desperately to avoid.

If you do not know any property owners in the market, then ride around in your neighborhoods and others like them and look for signs. You can attend a local Landlord Association or Real Estate Investors Association meeting. At these events you can network with local landlords and get the scoop on who is who in the management world.

CHAPTER 12

THE SALE

After your long road of finding a great property at an unbelievable price, getting the appropriate financing in place, going through the closing process, making repairs, managing the asset, getting it under contract, going through the buyer's closing process and finally getting the check from the closing agent. Success!

The day you sell the property should be fairly easy. Of course, there are steps that you need to take and things you need to keep a lookout for as you go through the closing process. But as I have said previously, the most important thing is buying the property at the correct price and doing the appropriate repairs at a reasonable cost. If you have accomplished these milestones along the way, then achieving your final goal should be relatively easy.

Let's discuss the sales process and what you will need to do to have a successful sale. The sale can be summed up in these steps:

Preparing the property to sell
Marketing the property
Negotiating offers
Appraisals and Inspections
Funding
Closing

Let's start with preparing the property to sell. There are a few different situations that you could be in right now. Potentially the best situation would be that you purchased the home a year and a day ago, you fixed it up when you purchased it and did a lease option with a tenant. Now the tenant is ready to exercise the option. You should not have to do anything to prepare the property for sale, or at least very little. The buyer is currently living in the home. He gave you a $5000 option fee one year ago that will be applied to the purchase price. The $5000 nonrefundable option fee along with the lease purchase contract that was implemented when you leased the property takes care of the marketing and negotiating offers. Also, since he is currently living in the home, he will probably not order any inspections. He should have a good idea of the condition. There will be an appraisal that will have to be ordered if the home is being financed, which in all likelihood will happen.

You would think that the appraisal would not be an issue at this point, and usually it is not, but I have had things pop up. For instance, a lease purchase that I mentioned earlier where I had to replace a roof because of an appraiser mentioning it being at the end of its useful life in the appraisal. When the FHA loan officer saw those comments, she flagged the loan, and I had to replace the roof to get the loan to go through. This was a $4000 solution. One thing I like to do to help get the appraisal to come in where it is needed is to have my Realtor assist me by pulling comps for the property and leaving them on-site for the appraiser to see.

Like everyone else, appraisers will follow the path of least resistance for the most part, and if you have legitimate comps that can be used and support the sales price, they will usually use them. This is especially important if you know of a sale in the neighborhood that will support your price, and it was not a typical sale through the MLS. This type of sale, such as a For Sale By Owner, will have to be proven by the tax records and can sometimes fall under the radar of the appraiser who is trying to turn out appraisals as quickly as possible.

Once you get past the appraisal hurdle, you move on to getting the loan closed. This can be an especially stressful process for both you and the buyer. In the situation we are currently going through with the lease/purchase, the buyer has already given you a $5000 option fee to be applied to the purchase price. He has been living in your home for a year and feels like the property is pretty much his. Now he has a banker implying he may or may not get the loan for the property. This is stressful. Tensions become raised easily. Here are a few things to help you get through this process with minimal stress.

Make sure that you have properly accounted for the money he has given you for the option fee of $5000 and the rent that he has been paying each month. I typically take a certified check for the option fee. This is a wise practice for you to follow. Make a copy of the check when you receive it and put it in the file. Ask him to take it directly from his bank account, if possible. If a friend or family member is giving him the money, I would have him place the money in his account before giving it to me. Of course, the check is going to be made out to the business that owns the property and promptly deposited into your business checking account. When you get the bank statement in the mail that has the deposit listed on it, I would make a copy of that statement and put it in the file as well. This keeps everything in one place where you can easily get your hands on it when the banker asks for it, and he will.

Your buyer will have to prove that the option money came from him when he goes to underwriting for the loan. The banker is going to ask for a copy of the check and the bank statement showing that the money came out of his account. I would ask him for a copy of this when he gives you the money, just to make sure you have it. I also stress to him at this point that he will need to keep a paper trail with copies of checks and statements for all the rent he pays. His rent payments will need to be made on time to help him get the loan. A bank is going to be reluctant to give him a loan if he has been paying his rent late to you. Everyone is going to be in a hurry to get the deposit in your hands so the tenants can move in at the beginning, so it will take some discipline on your part to make sure that all these details are taken care of. When the moment arrives, you will be thinking more about getting the people in the house and getting the deposit in your hands than you will about the sale to take place in 12 months; however, these few simple steps at this point in the process will be very valuable to you in the end. It may prevent you from losing a $20K, $30K or $40,000 profit.

Another thing to stress to your tenants/buyers at the beginning of the lease/option is that they need to correct any minor defects on their credit immediately and that if anything hits their credit during the 12 month lease that keeps them from getting the loan, they will forfeit the deposit they give you. This includes keeping their debt-to-income ratio in line. The debt-to-income ratio is the amount of monthly debt payments they have going out compared to the amount of monthly income they have coming in. Because the underwriting standards for these ratios change frequently, at least in the current financial environment, I would suggest you check with a local mortgage broker or banker for the current FHA, conventional and VA guidelines.

Two of the most frequent purchases which may lower the credit rating or raise the debt-to-income are furniture payments and car payments. Tenant/Buyers should not, as tempting as it is, go buy a house full of furniture on credit when they move into the house. They need to wait until they own the house and have closed on the loan. I have seen this come into play even when the buyers were not doing a lease purchase. Buyers will go buy a truck load of furniture on credit to be delivered the day they close only to find out that the loan is kicked back on the day of closing because of the last minute credit check. Do not let this happen to your buyers. This is your warning!

For some reason buyer/tenants also like to go get a new car as soon as they feel like they have a new house. I guess it is the feeling of upgrading their life and suddenly the old clunker just doesn't look appealing sitting in front of the new house. Please stress to them that this can cost them the house if they do it before closing. If you do not stress these seemingly little points to your potential lease/purchase clients, there can be a big surprise at the end of the option period. It is your duty to at least make them aware of the process. Many of your lease purchase buyers will assume the hard part is over when you let them move in. You must remind them that the real test comes at the end when the bank takes the loan and pays you off.

I have properties all over, so I always have the closing package mailed or shipped to me for my review and signing. I then get them notarized at the local bank and send them back with wiring instructions to my account. At this point, you will probably not have the settlement numbers in front of you. You will most likely get the settlement statement by fax or email to be signed and emailed or faxed back to the settlement agent. The deed will have to be original signatures and notarized so they will typically be circulated before the settlement date.

So now you have your deed signed, the settlement agent has your wiring instructions, the appraisal is back and came in at the sales price and your buyer has gone through the strenuous and frustrating loan approval process. You are finally ready to close! When the settlement agent gets the loan package and funds from the lender, he will settle the accounts, send a HUD-1 Statement for your review and wire the money to your account after the documents are recorded at the county courthouse. Remember, this is key. The buyers do not own the house until it is recorded at the courthouse. If you close late on Friday, then your buyers will not own the house until Monday. Not a huge deal if they are leasing the house but can be a big deal if they are not. You don't want the liability of them moving in before ownership.

Now let's assume that you bought a house with enough of a spread between your purchase price and the repair value that you can fix it up and sell it immediately. You close on the property, so now what? Well, as you probably know, you need to get the repairs completed as quickly as possible. The questions are where do you start and when do you market the property. I know from experience, your instant urge is to get the property right back on the market. Sometimes this is the right thing to do. Other times, it is not. You have to evaluate the current condition of the home and how it will influence the thinking of potential buyers.

If the home is in pretty good shape and you are really just freshening up the outside and replacing the carpet and paint to make it really look new, then it is probably safe to go ahead and have your Realtor put a sign in the yard. If the home looks bad, and even more importantly, if it smells bad from pet odor and other offensive smells, do not put up a sign and do not market the property until you get it complete. People will remember how the house used to be and not use their imagination like you and I. Remember, that is one of the key reasons we can be so successful when buying, renting and selling houses. The majority of the people do not have the vision that you and I have. If they did, they would have purchased the home before us and probably paid much more than we did. I know this concept sounds easy, but you will be tested when you close on a property. We all want to realize profit as soon as possible. Just remember our conversation here when the time comes.

Another reason you do not want your property marketed too early is because you do not want your potential buyers coming through the property when the repairs are under way. For one, it is a liability issue and two, they might mess up the wet paint or their new sweater in the wet paint, but even more importantly, you really don't want the contractors and the buyers talking without you present. I have some good contractors that I really trust, but even they hire a bad sub contractor sometimes. You don't want a sub using profanity or doing something that might offend the potential buyer, which happens very often. I have even heard subs say something negative about the property that is not even true! Why? I am not sure. Probably, because from their point of view, you are making all the money, and they are doing all the work. We know that this is not entirely the case, but please heed my advice and keep buyers and subs away from each other, especially when you or your Realtor is not with the buyers.

Which repairs should you do first? I usually start with getting the old carpet out of the house and hauling off any trash. At the same time, I get a crew working on the yard and landscaping. If your house looks abandoned from the street, you are inviting vandals and trespassers. The carpet usually smells bad and looks very bad; removing it gives the place an immediate change, usually for the better. I have found that if you have badly soiled carpet and you don't remove it first, it seems like the work from the subs is sub par. I think it subconsciously sends the wrong message. The down side of this is that if you use a specific sub for carpet, they will probably do a tear out for free if they are doing the installation on the same day. You may have to pay to get someone to remove the carpet before the installation, but in my opinion, it is well worth it.

You will probably get some neighbor interest as the sub contractors start to work on the property. Have your Realtor get cards on the counter and tell the subs they are there. After I get a home completely fixed up, I usually go door to door or have my Realtor send a mail out telling everyone in the neighborhood the home is available and the price. I usually invite them to an open house so they can see the house. This gets the neighbors on your side. They can replace the story in their head about the awful neighbors who had their dog chained up, had loud parties and never mowed their yard with the unbelievable job that you did fixing up the place. They are going to tell a story – that is what neighbors do. It can be for you or against you depending on how you handle neighbor relations.

Now you have the repairs completed, and you need to market the home. As you know, I always advocate the use of a Realtor. He only gets paid if he sells your house, and his fee is well worth it. Once you leave your kids' soccer game to go meet someone at the house on Saturday morning, and they don't show up, you will believe me. Make sure your Realtor has a marketing plan. You don't want a Realtor that is just going to stick up a sign and put the property on the MLS. You want to work with a professional. They should be actively using all the online tools to market your house. They should also be doing traditional marketing such as mail outs to prospects and open houses. Ask for a written marketing plan before you sign the listing agreement and make the plan an exhibit in the listing agreement. This is the best way to make sure what you are told gets done. If it doesn't, then he is not living up to his end of the contract.

When you are marketing the home, make sure you keep the yard cut and the inside clean. If you are having a lot of showings, then someone is going to have to use the bathroom at your home, so make sure the water is on. Also, have your Realtor check the home at least once a week to make sure it is clean. If it is not, have it cleaned. This is a small price to pay for losing a sale because the bathroom was left messy. No one wants to picture a messy stranger using the bathroom in her new home.

Now you have the home fixed up and listed with your Realtor. You start to get showings, and then the glorious day arrives in which an offer comes. You jerk the papers from your Realtor's hands and start to sign them as fast as possible, but wait a second. What message does that imply? Unless the offer is for full asking price and very tight terms, I always negotiate something, and I would encourage you to do the same thing. Let's put ourselves in the buyers' shoes. They are going to make an offer that is not quite what they are willing to pay so that when you come back with your counter, they have room to negotiate. But what if you don't come back with a counter? Then they are going to subconsciously think that they paid too much for the home. Even though they may be excited at first, when they get home that night, as they lie in bed, they are going to start to question whether they paid too much. This doubt starts to transform into other doubts such as, will the house even appraise for that much? Did we look at everything in the city in the price range and on and on. Avoid this! Negotiate on all but full price offers that have 30 days or less closings and no contingencies. Make your buyers work for the deal. They will appreciate it more.

You don't have to negotiate on price. It could be on closing or inspection dates, occupancy dates or any of the details of the contract. So if you don't want to scare the buyer with a price counter, pick other details to change.

One thing that you must always insist on having with your offer is an Approval Letter from the lending institution your buyers are going to use. I typically like to see these from a major bank, not a mortgage broker. I also look at the wording carefully because I want to make sure that the banker or broker has checked the buyers' credit and verified their income. If the letter of credit is subject to either one, I will reject it and ask for a letter that specifies that both have been audited and approved. The last thing you want is for your property to sit off the market and then not close. Other buyers get suspicious when a property has been under contract and comes back on the market. They think that the home inspection must have turned something up that was bad. Avoid having this perception by making sure you have a solid approval letter, not just empty words on the bank's letterhead.

CHAPTER 13

KEYS TO SUCCESS

In order to achieve success, we have to learn to control our mind, emotions and body instead of letting our mind, emotions and body control us. We have to realize that we are not our mind, emotions or body. They are our tools. We should use them to help us live out our destiny, not become a slave to them because we have not taken the time to discover our true Self.

Face your fears

We are our own worst enemy. Each and every one of us is capable of achieving unlimited success. We can do anything that we have seen another human being do and more. Fear is the only thing holding us back. Fear is our ego at work. Our ego works hard to protect itself and the result is fear. When we live a life with little fear, we don't have to have a large ego because we don't fear it being attacked. Without threat, the ego dissolves.

It is easy for us to tell ourselves that our fears are unfounded, but it is much harder to overcome those fears. One way to overcome our fears is to take one step at a time. Act in the face of fear. Simply, do what we fear doing. By taking small steps toward acting in the face of fear, we will eventually become comfortable in our new role, and the fear will fade. It might not disappear, but it will become less and less every time we do it. We will learn to control our fear rather than have our fear control us. This is one of the main things we must learn to be successful.

Fear comes from believing our perception is real instead of reality. We have a certain perception of ourselves, our lives and our world. When that perception is threatened, it produces fear. Our ego is our perception of who we are. When this perception is threatened, then we fear the threat. When we realize that we are much more than our ego, that our ego is a construct, then our fear starts to subside. One way to grow beyond the ego and, therefore, beyond fear, is through meditation.

Meditation

"Be still, and know that I am God" (Psalm 46:10).

In my opinion, meditation is the single most important thing you can do for your success and happiness in life. Meditating itself is not religious or philosophical in nature. You don't have to change your lifestyle or beliefs. I lead with the quote from the Bible above because sometimes people think that meditating is just for Eastern Religions, and that is not the case. Meditation is a way for anyone to get in touch with her true self. It is a process of going inside to find your true identity so you can present it to the world. Meditation will work for you regardless of your religious beliefs or lack thereof.

Meditating has changed my life tremendously. One of the best analogies that I have heard compares our soul to the ocean (if you don't like the word soul, feel free to use your own, source energy, for example). No matter what the surface of the ocean is doing, some days it is rough; others it is calm and smooth. The water underneath in the depths of the ocean is always present and always doing the same thing. It is not caught up in what is going on at the surface. It just exists in harmony below.

Just as the water in the depths of the ocean remains calm, so does your soul or your source. It doesn't get caught up in the rapid current of the mind thinking this thought one minute and the opposite the next. Its never ending chain of thoughts run on and on, jumping from one subject to the next, fantasizing about the future and fretting over the past. Continuously playing the movie of our lives on our mental screen, people coast through the present, barely realizing the present even exists, yet the present is all that does exist.

Meditation helps us cut through the thick fog that keeps us from experiencing the present that keeps us from experiencing true life. Meditation helps us detach from the movie and realize that we are missing the real thing! What we must all realize is that the past happened in the present, the future will happen in the present, the present is all there really is. There is nothing other than now. We need to focus our attention on the present so we can be the creative beings that we are. If we are walking around in the haze of replaying our past and fantasizing about our future, then how much of our focus and attention do we really have to devote to now, the present, where we actually live out our human experience?

We are all divine creatures that can accomplish anything! We can fulfill any desire we can create. The universe plays fair – it would not give us the ability to want something and then not give us the ability to realize it. We must connect with our soul, take control of our mind and body and direct it toward our destiny. We must clear our mind so that we can set our intentions, focus and energy to create, not rehash and fantasize. We need to create in this moment, the only moment we have, now in the present.

Meditation is our link to inner peace. Through meditation we can tap into our unlimited human potential so we can create and fulfill our destiny. Meditation is the practice of clearing our mind and joining our soul in the present. Trying to detach from the movie of the mind for just a second or two, we can experience the bliss of the present. The bliss of truly living. The bliss of pure potential. Here in the present, everything is perfect. There is nothing to stress about because right here, right now, all of our needs are met. Pause for a second and feel it. Place your attention on your breath. Are you breathing right now? Right now at this very second, you need nothing! We must train our minds to give us a break so we can dwell in this perfect place. The practice of Meditation is the not so secret passage way to our divine self.

If this all seems too far out for you, a little strange and uncomfortable, that's okay. Just consider it and give it a chance. When I first started to stumble onto the true "laws" of the universe, I thought they were strange as well. As a matter of fact, I almost took the audio book back that first started expanding my awareness. I was going through life thinking everything was cause and effect. I had not even noticed that I had lost my connection to God, my soul, my source. I am not talking about a religious God, but the God in us, our spirit. The spirit we connect to when we quiet our mind. Anyone can do this, and most successful people do, even though most don't talk about it. It doesn't take a special skill set or special knowledge. There are no clubs to join or rules to follow. All you need is you. All you need is to stop doing, stop moving and detach from your thoughts for just a few minutes and take time to exist. Feel the love in your heart and the peace in your soul.

A simple way to introduce meditation into your life is to take 10 minutes. Set the timer on your phone with a chime that is subtle, not abrasive. Close your eyes and simply observe your breath. When you notice that your thoughts are wandering, then gently place your attention back on your breath. You simply keep repeating this process. You are very gentle with yourself. This is not something that you can force. Be patient. It is like a pendulum swinging from your breath gently to thoughts and then gently back to your breath. Do this for 10 minutes until you feel the urge to sit longer. Increase the time until you get to 30 minutes. If you do this for 30 minutes twice a day, once in the morning upon awakening and once in the evening before leaving your office, then you will be amazed at how your life changes.

There is one person whom I must give a substantial amount of credit in helping me to understand the unseen forces that are influencing our lives every day, which engaged me in trying to understand this new world that awaits in our stillness. Karen is a beautiful person that I met while walking around an Earth Fare grocery store during lunch one day. For those of you not familiar with Earth Fare, it is like a Whole Foods. It is a large organic grocery store with a large natural remedy and cosmetic section. Karen was quietly standing at the end of the aisle when I walked by. She asked me if I would be interested in a tuning fork session. I had never heard of tuning forks, but after thinking about it briefly, I agreed to a ten minute session for ten dollars.

What happened in the next ten minutes amazed me. I sat down in the chair she made available in the aisle of the cosmetics in the middle of the grocery store. As people pushed their way around us to pick up their items for purchase, Karen asked me to close my eyes and uncross my ankles. She then explained that she was going to move the energy that had settled at the base of my spine back up to my head, so it could be used as creative energy.

As I sat there with my hands on my knees and my feet on the floor with my back and neck straight, Karen begin to ring the beautiful vibrating forks. First, one ear, then the next, then behind my head and down my back. She was working behind me as I sat listening to the sounds, wondering what, if anything, was happening. Then all of a sudden, it all changed. I had no expectations of what was going to happen, and quite honestly, I didn't expect anything to happen. But it did.

As she came over my head with the tuning forks, I saw bright, vivid flashes of white light shooting from the crown of my head. At first I reasoned that this was a bright light that was turned on in the store, and it was probably her moving in between me and the light that made it seem as though it was flashing. Then as she moved around in front of me, I started to see blue, purple and green lights flash up from below my head, as if coming from the ground. All of this amazed me. I didn't know what to think.

When Karen finished the 10 minute procedure, I opened my eyes to see the bright light that must have been turned on over my head, but it was not there. I realized that I had seen the energy that she was moving around. I had seen the different colors of the energy of my Chakras, a term I was not familiar with and a subject I knew nothing about at that time.

When I told Karen about my experience, she smiled and said that she was glad I enjoyed the treatment. She gave me her card and told me she did private sessions at several places around town. Every time I go back to the Charlotte area on business, I give Karen a call and have her share her gift. Karen woke me up to the fact that energy and its movement are very real, even though it is hard to detect if you are not living a conscious life. From that moment on, I wanted to know more about what happened and how I could access this world of energy for myself.

Set your Intentions

Some people set goals. I prefer to plant intentions. What's the difference? An intention is more about the seed of the thought, the beginning.

A goal is the destination, the end. An intention is about starting the journey but then allowing the journey to take a life of its own. A goal is about a predetermined destination. An intention is flexible. A goal is rigid. An intention keeps creativity alive during the whole journey. A goal has the potential to stifle creativity.

When you set a goal or declare an intention, you can only see things from where you are now. As you proceed along the path to your intended destination, you will gain new insights and see new things. Every step down the path will change your perspective of who you are, where you were and where you are going. Opportunities never anticipated will present themselves to you. Challenges never envisioned stand to alter your path. If you have an intention, rather than a goal, you are free to accept the opportunities and avoid unnecessary challenges. An intention is just that: you intend to do something, but if you see more clearly as you climb the mountains along your journey and your desires change, which they always do, then you can adjust your intention.

You use your intention just long enough for it to carry you over the next knoll. Then with your newly found perspective, your desires will change, and you are free to adjust your intent. I have heard people say that you can do the same with goals. It is not important whether you accomplish your goals but just that you set them. I agree with the principle but not with the expression of the principle. If you are setting a goal you don't anticipate achieving, I think you and your subconscious know this.

So why set something that is related to the end result? Why not set an intention for the journey? How much time will you spend at the end? How much time will you spend on the journey? Where is the real value in life? In the end result, reaching our goals? Or in the time spent on the journey? How many of you have reached a goal which has not brought you the happiness that you expected? How many of you have looked back on goals you have set in the past and thought, "Wow, I am sure glad I didn't get what I thought I wanted because I am much happier now in this current situation." I have done both. Usually, when we reach our goals, if we ever really do, our desires have moved on to bigger and better things. We get very little satisfaction out of the result, although the path that brought us there teaches us a great deal about our world and ourselves.

Set your intentions based on your current desires and realize these are only intentions. *Write them down* and imagine that you are planting the seeds of your desires. Declare your intent to manifest your desires. Once this is done, place your attention on your intentions. As you grow, you will develop new desires, and you are free to create new intentions. You are not abandoning your old intentions. They brought you to this point. They served their purpose. They took you along the path to the exact spot where you needed to arrive to realize your new desire and create your new intention. You are infinitely creative, truly free!

After you have realized your desire and set your intention, it is important to detach from the outcome. Spend your energy focusing on the present moment, not fantasizing about the future. If you are too attached to the outcome, you will miss the subtle hints of opportunity that present themselves along the way. Every day we have incidents and coincidences that provide us with the opportunity to move in a more fluid pattern. If we notice those coincidences and act on them free from detachment, we will live frictionless, happy lives. Everything we need to live abundant lives full of joy is presented to us every day. We just have to realize it and accept it. We have the habit of trying to remove all the uncertainty out of our lives because of fear of what will happen. What we are doing instead is creating a path based on fear instead of the path of our desires. This is the path of unhappiness.

Instead of fearing uncertainty, we need to embrace it! Uncertainty is fertile ground for new seeds to grow. Uncertainty is freedom from the past. Uncertainty is freedom to create. Uncertainty is the freedom to detach from the results or the outcome and go with the flow.

When you go with the flow, you stop swimming against the current by trying to force your way to your goals. You gently ride your desire and intention looking for opportunities and new desires, and when you see them, you embrace the new path. You thank the old path for carrying you this far, and without any regret or attachment to where that path was headed, you set your sights on the fresh fertile ground that now holds your new seeds of desire. Not worrying where it will end up or how it will work out, you set your intentions and head down the trail. You just focus on enjoying every step of the way and noticing the coincidence that opens the next door.

Have plans but take advantage of opportunities

"That is one of the tricks of opportunity. It has a sly habit of slipping in the back door, and often comes disguised in the form of misfortune or temporary defeat. Perhaps this is why so many fail to recognize opportunity." - Napoleon Hill

Life gives us all many opportunities to realize our dreams, to be the creative beings that we are and to fulfill our destinies, but most of us walk around in a daze stuck on a rigid schedule while our mind races with thoughts of the past and future, most of which are swirling around what other people think of us. What we must come to realize is that if we calm our minds, stay in the present and seize opportunities as they are presented, we will be much happier than trying to force everything into our predetermined mold, our schedule. This is one of the many things I love about being a real estate investor. My business doesn't depend on me to operate and make money; therefore, I am afforded the luxury of being able to take advantage of any opportunity that presents itself, whether that is taking a few minutes to talk to the elderly neighbor of the house I just purchased to hear about the progress of the neighborhood over the past half century, taking the afternoon to go to the beach with my kids because the sky is blue and the breeze is crisp or taking a week to go to the desert and meditate because I feel a calling to explore my inner-self.

Set your intentions on how you want to live and then let go. See what happens. Carpe Diem. Watch with amazement as your life unfolds. Keep your focus on the positive. Keep your mind centered through meditation. Stay open to the opportunities that present themselves. Stay flexible so you can take advantage of them. Don't be attached to the outcome.

If there is one single point that I want you to take away from this book, then it is this: security is an illusion. None of us know what is going to happen in the next seconds much less the next twenty years. People who say that starting a company or investing in real estate is risky don't understand risk. People who cling to a job they don't like because it makes them feel secure don't understand that nothing is secure. I am always amazed that most people think working for a large company is a more secure position than owning their own business. Yet, a person can be fired from his job overnight. Uncertainty needs to be embraced, not feared.

When you discover your desires, set your intentions and then become detached from the results, the entire universe opens up for you. You have a whole range of possibilities as things you were not expecting pop up and alter your course. If you embrace uncertainty, which you must do to be truly free, then every bump in the road opens the door to many opportunities. If you are stuck on the outcome, then you will try to force canned solutions on challenges that present themselves. This robs you of your creative energy. You will be trying to overcome fresh challenges with old ideas when new ideas will be presented to you at the time of the new challenges. Rigid attachment to outcome shuts out a whole range of ideas that are available to you. It robs you of your freedom. It stifles your creativity. What is security? Attachment to the known. What is the known? Our past. Therefore, security equals clinging to, or being attached to, the past. Being attached to the past offers no growth, just decay.

Uncertainty is creativity and freedom. Embracing uncertainty is being detached from outcome. Being detached from outcome allows you to be happy now. Uncertainty without attachment is true happiness.

Stay positive

Positive thinking keeps your overall attitude positive no matter what you are going through at the moment. This keeps you centered. If you are panicky and negative, then you are not open to creative ideas that can help you solve your problems. If you let your problems roll off you and you stay in a positive mindset, then you are in a position to act when options present themselves. And they always present themselves. As you read in the beginning of this book, I was laid off only four days after my daughter was born. A few paragraphs later I said getting laid off was the best thing that had ever happened to me. It's not that getting laid off is great in itself. It's not that you should say, "I am so glad I got laid off. Life is good." This would be absurd, especially in the moment that it is happening and you are facing all the pressure that the situation creates. It is not that we should be positive on the micro level – every single thing that happens is great and positive – but on the macro level. For instance, here are two very different reactions that you could have to the unfortunate situation of getting laid off. "I got laid off, that sucks. What am I going to do? Go collect unemployment? What if I never get a job? What if I lose my house, my wife?" or "I lost my job, that sucks, maybe this is a wake-up call, maybe I was wasting the best part of my life working for a company that didn't value me. What do I really want out of life? What is my purpose in life?"

In both situations, you are admitting that your current situation is not good. However, you can start running the video recorder in your mind rehashing the past and fantasizing about a doom and gloom future, or you can use the situation as a catalyst to stay present and keep your eyes open for the next opportunity.

It is not that being positive is going around with your head in the clouds and not being realistic about what is going on in your personal situation or the world. Being positive is having the underlying belief, or better yet **KNOWLEDGE**, that the universe is good and that we will all go through hard times, but those times will create new opportunities and grow our awareness. There can be no birth without death; there can be no renewal without decay. Things and situations deteriorate so there can be new things and situations created.

I am far from a scientist, but I have read and been told that quantum physics is proving that we create our own world through our conscious-ness. On the quantum level, matter does not exist; everything is a wave of energy. Particles can actually be in different places at the same time until they are observed by a human, and then they collapse to one place. There are infinite possibilities in every moment.

Now, I have had people say to me, "Kyle, if positive thinking really works, then why can't we just wish for a million dollars and get it?" And they are right, you can't just wish for a million dollars and it fall in your lap. (Although most people don't concentrate on getting a million dollars; they concentrate on their lack of a million dollars which pro-duces the lack.) You can plant the seed of desire for a million dollars. Then set your intentions to discover a way to get a million dollars. Next, let go of the outcome and trust in the universe to provide for you. Then one afternoon you buy a book at the book store that jumps out at you about making money, and you go to the seminar that you see advertised in the back of the book that teaches you how to make money. While at the seminar, you start a conversation with a guy who is sitting beside you. You find out he is at the seminar because his uncle has millions of dollars and told your new friend that he will give him as much money as he can competently invest. He can have all the money he makes over 6%, which will be paid to his uncle for the use of his money. You smile because on the airplane ride out to the seminar, you sat beside a guy who was flying out to the west coast to settle his brother's estate who owned a large portfolio of rental homes. The whole way out the brother fretted because he didn't have a clue how he was going to get rid of all those homes. The last thing this overwhelmed executor wanted to do was become a landlord. The seminar you both happen to be attending is how to find and fund income producing properties to make a high return with low risk. Now, I know you might be thinking, "This is way too good to be reality." I have had experiences that are not too far off from the one I just proposed.

When you keep a positive attitude, things like this will happen more often than not. Positive thinking is an evolution, a living, breathing thing, not a static thought toward one scenario. It's not, "I lost my job, that's awesome!" It's "I lost my job, that sucks, but what opportunities does that open?" When you see the door open, walk through!

Your thoughts are things

Everything that exists in this world began as a seed of thought. Our thoughts are living, breathing things that shape our world into what we see and perceive. If you see people as being kind and generous, then you too will likely be kind and generous; therefore, you will conclude that you live in a kind and generous world. If you have other thoughts about people, your world view will be shaped differently.

If you agree with this thought, then you need to be success conscious. That is, if you want to be successful, then you must think about how you can be successful and admire the qualities in other people who are successful. When you see successful people, you must feel good. When I was just starting to realize the truth of this, I would ask myself this question every time I met a person who I felt was more successful than I, "What are they thinking that is different than what I am thinking?" This is usually a very enlightening question to ask yourself. Typically, that is the only difference in the two of you.

Thoughts are vibrations. Our whole world is made of vibrations. Our brains become magnetized with the dominating thoughts that we hold in our minds. These thoughts create deep ruts in our mind and can repeat themselves over and over again thousands of times a day. These magnetic streams attract to us the forces, the people, and the circumstances of life which harmonize with the nature of our dominating thoughts.

We must become consciously aware of our thoughts. Allowing our unconscious reactions and repetitive thoughts to consume our lives will never get us to where we want to go. We must realize that we have a choice of the thoughts we think. Most of us don't really even realize that we have this choice. If someone tells us that we look like we have gained weight, we have a choice of how we feel and a choice about the internal dialogue that this comment starts within our brain. If someone tells us that we look like we have lost weight, we again have a choice of deciding what this means to us. To prove this just think, readers of this book are probably having different reactions to those two sentences right now. If you have been sick and lost weight rapidly and are now trying to regain your health, these comments will be taken differently than if you have been trying to lose weight for years and continue to feast and famine with no real success over the long run.

You see, we have total control over one thing. That is our thoughts. No matter what our circumstances, we can choose how we react and what we think. We must make sure that we are thinking thoughts that are constructive to where we want to go. Thoughts are way too important an asset to ignore and use unwisely.

Healthy Eating

Eating healthy and thinking positive have one very sly and important thing in common. Everybody, no matter how he eats or what he thinks, tells himself and probably tells others that he eats healthy and is positive. In our minds, we think we are eating healthy and thinking positively no matter what our actions really are. I only point this out so that you can be on the lookout for this point of view and observe yourself making these types of statements.

I have had a few defining moments in my life with regards to eating healthy. Some have been by conscious choice and some by unconscious choice. On New Year's Day, 2004, I found myself being rushed to the emergency room by my girlfriend, who is now my wife, in severe pain. I was 29 years old, I weighed 260lbs, and I was diagnosed with Pancreatitis.

For the next 25 days, I lay in a hospital bed being fed through a tube that ran into my right arm at the elbow. The only relief from pain was the Morphine drip that I milked for every drop I could get. The doctors said, what I perceived to be at the time a devastating blow, that I had caused this problem by being too overweight from eating fatty, rich foods and from drinking too much alcohol. Here I was at what I perceived to be the prime of my life being told by doctors that I had a disease that might cause me to never be able to live a normal life again, and I single handedly caused this situation by being a glutton and an alcoholic. Wow! Was that hard to take!

For the first 14 days or so, I lay in bed convincing myself that everything would be okay. That they couldn't be serious! I have to change my diet for LIFE! I can NEVER take one tiny sip of another alcoholic drink, and I have to work out to regain my strength and try to live as normal a life as one can expect in my situation. I had, they informed me, lost 1/3 of my pancreas to the disease that I would never regain.

After lying on my back for around 14 or 15 days, being hooked up to the machine that fed me and the other machine that numbed my body to the reality of what was going on, I had an epiphany, "I was going to have to change my life." More importantly, "I was going to have to change my way of thinking. My thinking about food, about social gatherings and about my whole life that I had planned out in my mind. There goes the cavernous wine cellar in the bottom of my castle-like mansion," I thought.

I tell you all of this to illustrate how hard it can be for us to see ourselves in an objective light. How much we can deny what is really going on in our lives. Mainly, how much it can take to change course. Most people would think that not drinking or eating certain foods would be given up easily by a guy in his twenties lying in a hospital bed being fed from a tube for two weeks! But not me. Until I had the "epiphany" moment, I actually lay there making excuses for what was happening. I was angry at the doctors for calling me an alcoholic. I was angry because they could not find out what was causing all this mess. I was angry because I would not observe myself in the situation I was in and take full responsibility for what was now happening.

It came to me all of a sudden in the middle of the night as I lay there watching the clock waiting for my next morphine drip to give me a little relief from my current life. "I am responsible for my life. I have to take control. I am not going to die at 29. I am not going to have everyone sit around feeling sorry for me saying, 'He drank himself to death.' I am not going to drink anymore, I am going to eat healthy and I am going to stay in shape. I am going to recover and lead a 'normal' life." Once I made these statements I started moving in the right direction. My mood changed dramatically. I still had many more agonizing nights and a long road to recovery, six months or more, but I knew that it was in my control and that I was going to be better than ever.

Now, seven years later, I can honestly say that my battle with Pancreatitis was the best physical thing that has happened in my life up until this point. Wow! Isn't that amazing! The thing that almost killed me. The event that cost me a normal life of eating without thought and drinking anything at any time I wanted. The event that put me through more pain than I can even now imagine. Spending a month on a feeding tube, 25 days in the hospital, losing so much strength that I couldn't walk up stairs without stopping and resting. The best thing that EVER happened to me! It changed my life by changing my thoughts which, therefore, changed my actions.

It is easy to ignore what is going on inside of you, especially when you are surrounded by others who are doing the same thing. I had friends who drank as much or more than I did. I ate no differently than everyone else in the restaurants I frequented. My life was no different than those around me.

Today, I think that some vegetarian diets are unhealthy! The funny thing is that now the people around me eat like I do. Some of them are the same people I dined with over seven years ago.

Exercise

I struggle just like others when it comes to staying on a consistent workout schedule. However, one thing is for sure. Exercise is more than physical. It has an effect on all aspects of your life. Exercise helps me relieve stress, achieve focus and remove toxins. It is always easier to sit at my desk and keep working on whatever has my attention than to get up, get dressed and go to the gym for a workout. It's all too easy to say, "I don't have time to work out." The reality is quite different.

If I take the time to work out, then it makes my whole day more productive. I feel energized and awake. I can focus more intently on what I want to get done. I don't feel restless. I sleep better, and most of all, I don't feel guilty for not working out.

I have tried all types of workout routines, but I find that a gym membership keeps me focused and motivated more than any other way. If I know that I am paying the membership every month, then I want to get my money's worth. Another favorite way to keep me going to the gym is to go out and treat myself to nice clothes. Then I have an incentive to keep the weight off. If I don't, my new jeans that I paid way too much for won't fit.

If going to a gym seems like a distant dream for you, then start by changing your diet. One thing I have noticed is that the more I work out, the better I want to eat. The better I eat, the more I want to work out. However, the opposite is also true. If I am not working out, then I start to not care what I eat. If I am eating fatty, processed foods, then I definitely do not feel like working out.

Be Balanced

Anything that is done repetitively over and over again for an extended period of time becomes uncomfortable. Think about it. If you have been walking all day, then sitting down on the couch feels great. However, if you have to sit on an airplane for ten hours, even first class starts to become extremely uncomfortable. It's all relative. It requires balance.

Exercise, sitting and even lying down can feel great when done for the right amount of time or when needed, but if you do any activities for too long, they change from pleasure to pain. Everything follows this same pattern. It is important to live in moderation and live a balanced life. It is easy to get caught up in the chase for money when times are good and the deals are flowing in. You know that if you just get one more deal, you can put another $20k or so in the bank account. It's sometimes hard to walk away, but you must. Don't sacrifice your relationships to add another check to the account, especially when you are already doing just fine.

If you have kids or a significant other, don't forget that having them around is probably why you are investing in the first place. Don't disrespect your relationship with them by answering the phone during dinner, even when it is the Realtor that is selling your big one this month. Remember, you are becoming an investor to gain freedom. Use the tools you are provided in this book so that your system works for you. Make it work on your terms. Don't fall victim to becoming addicted to the rush of making money to the point that it takes away from your other aspects in life.

Challenge your Assumptions and Expand your Awareness

The only way to grow, to evolve, is to change the way you look at the world right now. You can expand your awareness by being open to new ideas even if they feel threatening at first. As a matter of fact, this is the only way to grow. Pay attention to your reaction to new ideas. Do you react or do you respond? The definition of react is to exert a reciprocal or counteracting force or influence. The definition of respond is to make an answer.

The difference here is subtle, but very important. When you react to a new and different thought that challenges your assumptions, which is what we do in most cases, you are just counteracting the force or influence of that new thought. This is a fear based reflex. You feel threatened, and you counteract with force. When you are responding, you are "making an answer." You are creating. You are considering the new information, blending it with your old assumptions and creating a totally new answer of thought. When you respond, you are open to change. You are open to expanding your awareness. A response is based on openness, not fear.

Make sure that you take a moment in between the time you hear a comment, or have a thought, and evaluate what you have heard or thought. If you react instantly in your mind, notice that fact. What are you saying to yourself? Is it a loving and open comment or a negative fear based comment? Why? More than likely, it will be a reactive fear based comment if it is something new to you or something that challenges a current belief or perception. It will be a more positive and open response if it is something you already find agreeable.

If you stay in the repetitive pattern without being aware of it, then you can never grow. You can never learn. If you only are open to things that you already know and agree with, then there is no reason to keep searching for new knowledge. You are just trying to find justification for what you already believe. But would you need justification if it were true?

Be open; pause before responding. Don't go through life being reactive. Challenge your assumptions and expand your awareness. You will evolve into a more expansive and understanding person. Just because someone gives you a half price offer on a house you are trying to sell and tells you that you are crazy for asking that much, doesn't justify your countering back that it's worth every penny and that he must not be able to afford it. Seek to understand why he is offering what he is. Why does he feel the way he does? Then be open to a solution. It may be that his Realtor is a relative who only sells houses to other relatives (meaning once every few years) and saw on the evening news that you can buy houses for half price because of the current market (which is all true!).

If you had reacted to his comments, then you would have probably made him mad, and the deal would be dead. However, if you have your Realtor explain to the buyers that they may be able to buy a foreclosure that needs repair for a deep discount, but your firm-priced home is ready to be lived in and qualifies for government financing, you may be able to save the deal.

Faith

A very important factor in my success has been my faith that everything is going to work out for the better. There are many times I have gone into a new situation not knowing how it was going to work out, but I have pressed on knowing that it was the right thing to do at the time. We must have faith in others, faith in our ideas and ultimately faith in ourselves.

A recent example that I have mentioned earlier in this book was when I started to buy rental properties. I had no clue how I was going to buy rental properties with no job and very little money, but even more than that, I did not know how I was going to make enough money to support my family and my other business obligations by renting houses. If I had stuck with pure logic, I would have calculated that I could make a hundred to two hundred dollars a month per property. If I had listened to the bankers and not pressed on, I would have only thought I could buy three properties. If I had just used logic and not had faith that it would all work out, I could easily have talked myself out of moving forward before I even got started.

Here is the way I see the world working. If you have faith and move in the direction of your dreams, then doors will open as you go along. As they open, you must seize the opportunity and have faith in the newly created path. As you continue down the path, you must be steadfast in your faith. When you meet obstacles, keep your faith. Keep moving forward and look for other doors to swing open.

If you try to figure it all out from the beginning, you will not be able to see the whole picture. As you continue down your chosen path, you will learn valuable lessons along the way. Those lessons will help you see things differently. They will change your perspective. You do not have to know how it will all work out when you start down any road in your life, financial or otherwise. All you need is enough information to get started and the faith that we can figure it out as we go along. As you move along, gain new information and gain new perspectives, then we adjust our plans and keep moving ahead with faith that this is the best way right now. We also remain open to new and better ideas as we go.

I can look back on my life up until this point and credit my faith with helping me get through many transition points. After only a year and a half with the company I went to work for out of college, I left to try a different position with another company. Both positions were sales positions, and both were 100% commission. I left a position where I was making $75,000 a year. Not bad for a recent college graduate in 1998. I left to pursue a more attractive position in a different industry. I worked at my new position for 4 months without making a dime. My savings dwindled to my last $4000 dollars. I did not see a paycheck in site, so I decided to go back to my old industry.

Instead of going back to work for the company I left, I started a company to help solve one of its big problems. I became a vendor to a vendor of the company and started making as much money as I was before, but this time I was working out of my house on my own schedule. I had traded a job working seven days a week for a job working whenever I wanted via a failure at a job I thought was the next big thing. I could have never predicted all of these twists and turns from the beginning!

I had faith that I could learn sales and make enough money to support myself at a 100% commission position right out of college and took it. At the time, I had no money. I mean none. I think I had about $600 in my checking account, and my parents had given me fair warning that once I graduated from college, I was absolutely and completely on my own! In the first four weeks on the job, I sold four homes producing a commission of over $14,000! Although I never topped that first month, as I mentioned earlier, I ended up making $75,000 over my first twelve months.

I could have held on to that position, clutching to it as hard as I could. I was making more than anyone I knew at my age. Instead, I sat in my office reading the Wall Street Journal every day dreaming about playing in the booming IPO world of the late 1990's. Yeah, I was making good money, but I was working in the low tech world of manufactured homes, commonly referred to as mobile homes. I wanted more sizzle, and I had faith that I could obtain what I wanted. So after working for a year and three months at my first after-college job, I started interviewing with other companies.

I was hired by a corporate branding company. I went down to the interview pumped up for the job. I never doubted I was going to get the position. I had complete faith. As I parked my car and walked down the downtown streets, I smiled as I passed groups of men and women dressed in business suits. "This is it! This is me!" You see, I had spent the last few years in the foothills selling homes to everyday people in a sales trailer on a gravel lot on the side of a busy state road. The lure of fine clothes and city streets made my head spin.

On my ride up the elevator to the 41st floor, I felt my stomach drop. I was way out of my element. I approached the large double doors to the entry and gained my composure as I walked in and gave a flirty hello to the attractive young lady behind the receptionist desk. After a quick phone call to announce my arrival, I was asked to sit and wait, which I did.

After the interview, I was pumped up and ready to go. I knew that I had the job. Nothing was said to give me this confidence, but deep down, I knew. I drove straight up to the sales center where I worked, about an hour and a half away, and asked to have a few minutes of my manager's time. I told him that I would hand in my resignation letter tomorrow. He informed me that he didn't need me to work my two week notice, wished me luck and that was the end.

As I pulled out of the parking lot, I got the warm feeling in my stomach that I get every time I start a new chapter in life. A feeling that is now an old friend. The feeling of anything being possible. The feeling of leaving the old and starting the new. A feeling of growth and renewal. A feeling of faith in change!

A few weeks after my initial interview, I was called to a second interview and given the job! I was extremely excited. This wasn't the mobile home business! No more walking the gravel lot showing homes that were hot in the summer and cold in the winter. No more stressing over how I was going to get someone financed who had never repaid anyone. This was the big time!

The first day I put on my suit and smiled as I rode the elevator up to the 41st floor. I walked in and felt proud that I was now working in the city, among 30 or so other branding consultants. After a half day of introductions, I was given a list of companies 10 or 20 pages thick and shown to my cubical, my first and last cubical.

I was instructed to call at least a hundred contacts a day. The companies listed were mine. I was to use the internet to research them, find contacts and call to get their business. The business I was searching for was naming and creating identities for products, companies, services, technologies etc. and helping them trademark what we created. I couldn't wait to get started!

After a few months and 5000 or so calls, I realized that my new career path was not for me. By this time, the city location and tall building with a long elevator ride had lost its mystic. I longed for a lazy afternoon at the sales center with my feet up on the desk reading the Wall Street Journal. I longed for a real office and not a cube. Most of all, I longed for a pay check!

Feeling defeated, but keeping faith that everything would work out somehow, I cleaned out my desk one night when working late leaving the key on top. Now I was down to my last $4k, and I knew I had to figure out something quickly. I called one of my friends who hired me when I graduated from college to see what he was doing. He had changed companies about the time I had left. He was now managing a sales center for a competitor. I went to his office the next day, not really looking for a job, but just to visit my old environment to see if it would work now that I had a different perspective.

As we talked, he asked me if I wanted to move. I told him that I liked Charlotte and would like to stay there. He mentioned a friend who had set up a vendor relationship with our old company. The vendor was now trying to find subcontractors to help him. The subcontractors were brokering repossessed mobile homes for banks. My friend said that the banks were looking for someone to represent another city, so if I was willing to talk with them, that might be an avenue. I liked the idea! Owning my own company. Not having a set schedule. Being my own boss. I went to see them.

After our meeting I was amazed to find that they did need someone in the Charlotte area. I took my last $4k and bought equipment to start the business. Within no time I was making $6k plus a month, but now I was playing golf two or three times a week and staying out to 2 A.M. drinking and partying with whomever I could find to join! I was single,

25, and operated the business off my dining room table. At the time, this seemed like heaven!

My unusual twist of events had placed me back doing what I was before – selling manufactured homes. Now I was just doing it for banks instead of the manufacturer and doing it for myself instead of a corporate "parent."

I tell you this story so you can see how faith took me from one situation to another which ended up being much better in the long run through what seemed to be failures and bad decisions at the time. This is just one small example from my life. I can tell you many more. I am sure that if you examine your own life with an eye toward faith, you will see how you were on the road to your biggest success when you thought you were failing. You succeeded because you kept faith in yourself and continued to move forward by making the best decisions you could make at the time.

There is no way I would have ever known how this situation would have ended from the perspective I had when working for the mobile home company. Even if you had given me the opportunity to start my own company to sell repossessed mobile homes, I would have turned it down at that point. I would have thought, "Are you crazy? Leave the manufacturer to sell dirty used homes? How will I stay in business?" However, at just the right time, the opportunity presented itself. I just had to have the faith to take the first step when I felt the decision was the best for me. The rest works itself out as you go along. Look for examples of this in your own life and think of them before you decide to let your next idea or dream pass without acting on it.

Remember that having faith doesn't mean that you keep doing the same thing thinking, "It has to get better at some point." That is wishful thinking. You have to look for new opportunities and take action when needed. Having faith is not keeping blinders on to other options; however, it is having confidence in your ability to make the correct decisions and to make those decisions turn out positively. Sometimes they turn out to be beyond your wildest expectations.

CHAPTER 14

MORE THAN MONEY

Building wealth has helped me to live a happier life. By investing in income producing properties, I have had the freedom to create the Free Me Forever! Wealth Creation system, to write books, to give seminars, to produce CD's, and to design training programs. I have had the freedom to grow as a person, the freedom to share my experiences with others, the freedom to examine what is really important in life. This freedom is what is really of value, not the money. The money is just a tool for the freedom the money provides.

When you free up your day, you start to use some of the time to ask yourself very fundamental questions – questions that lead to an increased awareness about what makes you happy. We have all seen rich people who are far from happy. Why is this? I think it has to do with how we spend our time.

Time is what we all really crave – time for ourselves, time for our loved ones, time to examine what we want in life. Many of us just hurry through life trying to make ends meet or meet the next deadline or even trying to add another zero to the end of our bank account without ever taking a step back and asking ourselves, "What does it all mean? Why are we doing what we are doing? Are we really getting what we want out of life?"

By putting a system in place to help you create wealth, like the Free Me Forever! system, you will free yourself from the daily grind. You will create new income streams as you buy rental homes and buy and sell fixer uppers. You will create companies to hold your properties and operate your properties. You will create value buying houses that need repair and fixing them up.

You will free yourself to grow as a person. You will have time to spend studying the things you have always wanted to study. As you develop yourself, you will feel your perception start to change, and you will free yourself even more. You will find that your growth in itself makes you happy and more fulfilled.

As your creations grow, you will want to share your experience with others, just like I am doing now. I had absolutely no intention of writing a book and teaching others when I started investing back in 2007. If you had told me that I would be writing a book about investing and teaching students around the globe how to invest, I would have thought you were crazy. Now, this is my reality. My small real estate investment business has now grown into a global company. You will follow this same path. As you develop yourself, you will feel the urge to share as I have. It's our obligation to help others live a better life. This obligation is pure joy to fulfill.

By sharing with others, you will recognize your love for humanity. You start to see the positive in people. You realize that everyone has tremendous potential. Everyone is doing the absolute best he knows how to do from his current situation. You learn that by giving people a nudge in the right direction, their lives can take off in new and exciting ways.

As you start helping people, you start to feel a deep sense of love. You start to accept others for who they are and move closer and closer to unconditional love. When you start to experience love on a large scale, then you are truly free. You learn that there is nothing in this world to fear. You can simply be *FREE.*

Making money is not required to take this journey from where you are now to being free. Not all people require a passive income or wealth. You *do* have to spend time to reach this high level of freedom. Freedom from fear. A life of love.

You have to spend time asking yourself questions about who you are and what you want out of life. I found that I needed to develop wealth so that I could lift my head up from the day-to-day activities that consumed my life up until that point. If I had not found a wealth building formula to pull my head up, I could easily have gone through my entire life fearing poverty – working my life away to escape this fear.

CHAPTER 15

THE NEXT STEP

So what is your next step? Was this book enough to get you pointed in the right direction? Do you need more support? What will make you happy in life? Are you working too hard for too little? Are you burning time that you can never get back? Are you missing the precious moments with your spouse, significant other or children while trying to make ends meet? Do you spend your time doing things that are not really helping you achieve your end goals? Do you know your end goals? Your intentions? Your Purpose? Are you living your life on purpose or by default?

If you take the time to answer the above questions and revisit them every week or so, then that in itself will provide you with clarity and help you to start creating your own life rather than living the default life that leaves you feeling frustrated and empty.

As I have mentioned before, this book seems to be about real estate on the surface, but it is really about living a happy and fulfilled life. Real estate was my vehicle to discovery. I think that it is a very accessible vehicle which anyone can use, so I offer you the system I created. I also have a three day seminar, a very in-depth home study course and various audio and video programs that can aid you in your pursuit of wealth and happiness. I am adding courses as this book is going to publication, so make sure you check the website, *www.freemeforever.com*, to get updated offerings and see when I am coming to a city near you.

Thank you for spending your time with me. Remember, if you keep doing the same thing, you will keep getting the same results.

www.ingramcontent.com/pod-product-compliance
Lightning Source LLC
LaVergne TN
LVHW091152080426
835509LV00006B/655